Her Space

*Enjoy
Marilyn A. Jessen*

Her Space

She Sheds, Back Rooms and Kitchen Tables

Marilyn Jessen

Bateman

Text © Marliyn Jessen 2016

Published in 2016 by David Bateman Ltd
30 Tarndale Grove, Albany, Auckland, New Zealand

www.batemanpublishing.co.nz

ISBN 978-1-86953-944-3

This book is copyright. Except for the purpose of
fair review, no part may be stored or transmitted in
any form or by any means, electronic or mechanical,
including recording or storage in any information retrieval
systems, without permission in writing from the publisher.
No reproduction may be made, whether by photocopying
or by any other means, unless a licence has been obtained
from the publisher or its agent.

Book design: Cheryl Smith
All internal photographs by the author except those listed
on page 294
Printed in China through Asia Pacific Offset

This book is dedicated to the two women in my life with whom I share creative DNA.

My mother, Margaret Voyle, who fostered in me a love of all things creative, and

My daughter, Brie Jessen-Vaughan, who is putting her own unique, personal stamp on our family's creative traditions.

Contents

Introduction 9
Carving a Lifestyle — Liz McAuliffe 12
Creative Get Up — Sandra Thompson 17
A Stitch in Time — Jo Dixey 21
A Gift from Jess — Sandra Hosking 26
Fleurs du Mal – 'Flowers of Evil' — Vanessa York 30
With Thanks to My Teacher — Dagmar Dyck 34
Letting the Madness Out — Julie Jensen 38
A World in Miniature — Bev Johnstone 42
Memorable Moments — Christine Sedgwick 45
Soul Sisters — Dhyana Muir & Reina Cottier 49
Getting Started Creatively 55
Baroness Ditzy von Karbon — Gin Clay 58
Lady Lavinia Laudanum-Swoon — Linda Stephenson 61
Master of Dolls — Cindy Harvey 65
Fresh Talent, Big Dreams — Georgia Lines 70
Precious Cargo — Jan Fraser-McKenzie 74
Quilter of the Glen — Helen Hagan 77
Through the Looking Glass — Karen Anderson 81
Lighting the World — Clare Wimmer 85
Mountain Dreaming — Susan Flight 89
Staying Passionate about Being Creative 93
Life's Too Short — Jill Matthew 97
A Day at the Races — Monika Neuhauser 101
Skid Row — Gerlinde Weinzettl 105
A River at My Door — Nynke Piebenga 109
Māwhitiwhiti – a Weaving Legacy — Kahutoi Te Kanawa 113
A Magic Garden — Judi Brennan 117
Hūtarau – 100 Hūia — Bernise Williams 122
Chisel in Hand — Anna Korver 126
Champagne She Cave — Barbara Valintine 130
Accidental Art — Heather Rees 134

Creating Your Very Own Her Space 139
Set in Concrete — Sue Mabin 142
Right Place, Right Time — Rhonda Lidgard 146
Alchemy and Magic — Su Hendeles 150
Artmosphere — Sally Maguire 154
At the Crossroads — Tracy White 158
Her Space, Any Place — Sue Lund 164
Goodbye, Proper Job — Rachel Pfeffer 169
Raising the Flag — Paula Coulthard 173
A Doll's House for Adults — Anthea Crozier 177
Wearable Art to Art to Wear — Jan Kerr 182

The M Words — Marketing and Money 187
Grove of the Summer Stars — Pamela Meekings-Stewart 194
The Makers — Annie Collins, Vaune Mason, Gemma Miller, Natalie Salisbury 198
In the Quartermaster's Store — Jane Brimblecombe 202
A Window to the Soul — Rebekah Codlin 206
A Room with a View — Christine Boswijk 211
No Fixed Abode — Jenny Birdling 216
For Every Occasion — Bev James 222
Stash Palace — Jane van Keulen 226
Carving a Legacy — Kristy Wilson 230
Hand Cranked — Jacquie Grant 234
A Story of Dolls — Raewyn Parker 238

Working with a Gallery 243
Painting Their Way to a Better Life — Mary Stevens & Jo Banham 246
Safety Gear Required — Hannah Kidd 252
In God's Name — Sister Annette 257
Watching the Wildlife — Madison Drinkall 261
When the Bell No Longer Rings — Gina Tatom 265
Out of the Blue — Mary Monckton 269
Singing with Life — Sue Wademan 273
Lavender's Blue — Karen Rhind 277
Ever-expanding Journey — Kylie Matheson 281
Totally Stumped — Jo McCraw 285
Halfway around the World — Laire Purik 289

Photo credits 294
Acknowledgements 295
About the author 296

Introduction

New Zealand women are extraordinarily creative. They knit, they weave, they write and they build. They are jewellers and milliners, painters and sculptors, crafters and collectors. We know them as daughters, partners, wives, and mothers, and as carers and career women who juggle busy lifestyles and multiple roles, while satisfying their deepest desire to create. Our lives are enriched by their work. These women, in ever increasing numbers, are making their own oasis or haven, a *Her Space*, in which to do what I believe comes naturally to us all — being creative.

Over the past year I have had the privilege of stepping into the *Her Space* of over 60 artistic, creative and inspirational women, who are living and loving life by following their passion. They are some of the busiest women I have met, and yet they manage to carve out time to do what undoubtedly comes from the heart. Some are in the early stages of their creative journeys, working at a day job and creating in their precious spare time. Some have taken the leap of faith and given away the security of a steady income to do what they love, hoping and believing that the money will follow. And there are a few who have been at it for long enough to know that it is financially sustainable, even if things do get a little scary along the way.

Regardless of the stage in their journey, these extraordinary women have been incredibly welcoming, openly sharing their spaces, their talents and their genuine excitement for what they do. Each woman's *Her Space* is truly unique, ranging from small to large, basic to lavish, and from kitchen tables to back rooms, garages and 'she sheds' tucked down the garden path. Some have dedicated spaces, which they confine themselves to, while others spread out and infiltrate their whole living area. Some have the luxury of finishing a session and leaving everything out for the next time, while others have to pack it away to make room for the next meal or the relatives coming to stay. Some are well organised, some are messy. Without exception, all of the ladies have created a space that works for them, rich in inspiration with photos, drawings, colour swatches, clippings and quotes, together with mementos and collectables, gathered over the years for sentimental reasons. Collectively these bits and pieces, and precious keepsakes put a personal stamp on each lady's space.

I refer to them as extraordinary and they are. But they are also ordinary women made extraordinary by doing what many of us silently yearn to do: to follow our passion. They're not waiting for someone else to give them permission or for the perfect time or place. All have faced challenges, physical, financial and emotional, but they do it anyway. They talk about taking time out, investing in themselves, and sharing their talents with the world. Some talk of the extraordinary power of creative endeavour to heal and give meaning to life, even in its roughest moments.

I am inspired by every one of the people I have interviewed. Their photos are on my pinboards, and when I look at them, at least on a daily basis, I am reminded of the gems of information, the insights, and the new perspectives I have gained. Without exception I came away from every interview feeling richer for the experience, and I am truly indebted to the women whose stories lie within.

It is my hope that in reading this book you will be inspired to tap into and extend your own personal creativity. From what I have seen there are three secrets to success: take a risk and give it a go; work at it, as it takes consistent effort; and put yourself out there, share your work with the world and listen to the feedback that follows. Even then it may not work like you want it to, but as each of these women would tell you, they are happier and better people because they are giving it a go. That to me is success.

As well as each lady's story I have added some 'food for thought' pages. If you are at the beginning of your journey, yearning to be creative, you might like to check out the 'Getting Started Creatively' section. If you've already started, but are finding it hard to maintain your creative momentum, there may be some helpful suggestions in 'Staying Passionate about Being Creative' or 'Creating Your Very Own Her Space'. Many of us dream of turning our creative passion into a full-time job; 'The M Words — Marketing and Money' may provide some insight. These pages are a combination of my experience in marketing, and in teaching creativity through music, photography and film, combined with the knowledge and insights from each creative's story. If you are thinking of approaching a gallery, you should also check out 'Working with a Gallery', which contains great advice from experienced gallery owner, Sally Maguire from Artmosphere in Waipawa.

Wherever you are on your creative journey, I wish you every success. I hope you will find, within these pages, someone to identify with, something new to try, or someone to be inspired by, and above all that you get excited about creating your own unique, inspirational, and productive *Her Space*. May it truly nourish your soul.

Celebrating all things creative,
My warmest regards,

Marilyn Jessen

Liz McAuliffe
Kohukohu, Northland

Carving a Lifestyle

Nestled on a hill overlooking the beautiful Hokianga Harbour, with views to Rawene in the south and Motukaraka in the west, is the studio and home of wood carver and artist Liz McAuliffe. For Liz, who draws her inspiration from nature, it is her sanctuary, a place where creation, in the spiritual sense, meets creativity. From the moment you open the gate, you are treated to a visual feast of lush, natural gardens. As you venture further up the driveway, the skyline opens up to reveal a stunning pole house built in natural timber perched on the hill, and if you pause and look across the treetops you get to see the magnificent harbour views, which Liz awakens to every day.

The hub of Liz's home is a large hexagonal area that serves as dining room, lounge and kitchen. Off to the left is a large open veranda overlooking the garden, with a smaller workshop to the side. It is here that Liz creates her magic, carving and painting a wide variety of everyday objects found in the garden — pōhutukawa leaves, kauri cones, kōwhai pods, flax seeds, lotus pods, and kauri snail shells — and treasures collected from the beach: scallop shells, sand dollars and starfish. Each is individually carved and painted to create life-like replicas that range from hand sized to more than two metres tall.

The veranda is a large space with a macrocarpa table where we sit to enjoy the sunshine that pours in through the large windows and roof skylights. In the far corner is Liz's painting table, where she has been busy painting large canvas leaves in beautiful autumn colours. From this corner Liz can gaze out at the garden or across the treetops to the harbour, listening to the rhythms of daily life — the car ferry as it comes and goes, the birds and cicadas, and the cars that pass on the road below. They are distant and reassuring sounds, which Liz says make her feel connected to the outside world. 'I'm a bit of a reclusive person. I like to feel connected, but I don't need to socialise a lot.'

To the right of where we are sitting is another large table, which is covered with a collection of another of Liz's signature works — her *Philately Will Get You Everywhere* postage stamp series. Carved in MDF, they feature a huge variety of images ranging from native flowers, to scenery, to religious icons. True to life there are the wrinkles and torn edges. 'I see the detail in everything,' says Liz.

Beside the table is the drill press, which is so vital for creating the intricate perforated edges of the stamps. This is one of two drill presses Liz owns, the other residing in the workshop directly behind the table, along with a bandsaw and a range of Dremel carving tools. 'I don't do hand carving. I use machinery to speed things up: chainsaws, Arbortech attachments on angle grinders, power carvers, sanders, and drills. I like to get results quickly. The really messy stuff I do under the house, wearing a powered respirator. Then it comes up to the workshop

for the finer carving. When I've finished carving it goes out to the deck to be painted. I live amongst my art. I like to be surrounded by it.'

So how did Liz get started? Ten years ago, she signed up for a one-year visual arts course in Opononi, under the tutelage of Sue Daly. Run in conjunction with Work and Income the course was designed to assist local artists to turn their artwork into a full-time career. During the course Liz had a chance to try her hand at a variety of mediums including jewellery, painting and sculpting. It was Dr Glen Hayward, a renowned sculptor, who inspired Liz to focus on her carving.

Starting with small objects from home, her first being a lotus pod, she was encouraged to extrapolate her ideas, scaling up to large carvings and cross-sections. After a visit from Mobile Art Renters, an organisation that rents art to business and private customers, Liz was encouraged to create oversized artworks, which could be used in commercial foyers — among them a 1200 mm scallop shell and a kōwhai pod almost as tall as her. Working with a business mentor and with the backup of a Work and Income grant, Liz took the leap of faith, mortgaging her home to provide an income for herself while she built up stock and started to market her work through galleries and her website.

Liz held her first exhibition at Village Arts, the local Kohukohu gallery. Other exhibitions and commissions followed with her work now in national and international collections, including work in Italy, Denmark, Germany and Australia.

The year 2015 was an exceptionally busy one with Liz shipping out work for over 40 exhibitions, art shows and showcases. On the wall of the workshop is a large blackboard where Liz planned out her year's work. Although it is now 2016, Liz has left it there. 'It is a reminder of what I have achieved for the year. I was really focused. But this year I want to be more balanced in my lifestyle. I'm also trying out new materials, one of which is Perspex. It's a harsh material to work with. It's not as forgiving. I'm not sure yet if I like it.'

Already the hard work of last year — and the previous 10 years — is paying off, with six sculptures sent to a London design apartment, a commission for a large work and a three-month residency in Denmark. 'The future is so exciting. The feelings of nervousness and trepidation, and questioning "will it work?" It keeps me stretching my skills. I never want to lose that sense of wonder.'

Liz explains her work process. 'I'm constantly looking at nature, and bringing pieces home. I watch how the light creates dappled shadows and I incorporate that into my work. I sketch the small pieces in my book, and then plan out what I'm going to do, scaling them up to the final size. I don't work with music or the radio. I like to hear the sounds of nature, and my own thoughts.'

Liz is very organised. She makes a month's meals in advance and freezes them, so that she can eat without interrupting her workflow. She also limits her time spent on the computer. 'I'm purposely creating a quiet, contemplative life,' she says. 'This space suits me. It's familiar and comfortable and I keep it well organised. I have a sense of belonging here and a sense of excitement. It reminds me of what I can do and still want to do. And the view from the doorway is my absolute inspiration. To create is good. I practically live in my studio.'

Sandra Thompson

Parekura Bay, Bay of Islands

Creative Get Up

It was just over 30 years ago when Sandra Thompson and her partner sailed into the Bay of Islands and dropped anchor in Parekura Bay. Having left Waiheke Island two years before, they had no deliberate plans to put down roots, but one thing led to another and they purchased two acres of bare land with stunning views across the bay and out to Urupukapuka Island. Making the most of the picturesque setting, they designed and built their own home, completing all the building work themselves with the exception of the electricals. This same DIY talent has seen Sandra build a successful art-clothing business, making one-off garments from felted or woven wool and silk. The garments are absolutely exquisite and reflect a love of colour, and flair for design. Having seen them on her *Creative Get Up* website, I was excited to meet her and see her workspace.

Clad in dark green corrugated iron, Sandra's studio looks like a typical Kiwi farm building, but there is nothing typical about the work that goes on inside. On the ground floor alongside the car garage is the fabric making area. Sandra's fabrics start life as undyed merino slither, long strands of carded wool, or silk fibre. The raw fibres are wonderfully soft, and the silk has a beautiful lustre even in its raw state.

There is a large table in the centre of the room, which is used to lay up the fibre for felting, and to the left of this is an eight-shaft weaving loom. Opposite the loom is a sink bench where Sandra hand-dyes the slither or yarn. 'Felting can be a messy business,' says Sandra. 'I dye the fibre first and then, if it's a coat, I start by laying up the silk fibre, adding the wool fibre on top, blending in the colours. It evolves as I go. For a coat I have to make two or three lengths to get enough fabric, because the fabric shrinks up to thirty per cent in the felting process.'

Sandra has a love of rich blues and greens and vibrant autumn shades, all colours she sees around her in her everyday world. Sandra also hand-dyes her yarns for weaving, including hand-painting her warp threads to get an ever changing colour base throughout the woven piece of fabric.

Once the fabric is complete it's off upstairs to the sewing room. This is a large, airy space with plenty of natural light. The walls are painted in a vibrant blue with yellow window trim. In the centre of the room is a large cutting table with a beautiful blue and purple fabric destined to become a jacket, which, along with her ripple scarves, have become her signature pieces. There is a single-needle industrial machine, an overlocker and a domestic Bernina machine she uses for her freehand stitching. Looking around the room you get a sense of Sandra's creativity. In addition to the wool and silk garments there

are flax creations and her latest work made from multi-coloured, heavy duty fishing nylon. 'The nylon comes from the fishing boats. I'll probably exhibit this one in a "trash to fashion" show,' she explains.

Even the display models are Sandra's own creations, made from flax fibre, which she has moulded onto a stretch fabric with a mixture of PVA and wallpaper glues. 'It took a lot of experimenting to find the right mix to cope with the humidity in a shop, and to be rugged enough to put up with the wear and tear. I only started making them as galleries told me they didn't have a way to display my garments.'

Sandra describes herself as having been on a textile journey the whole of her life. As the fourth child in a family of eight there were always buttons to sew on and mending to be done. These became Sandra's responsibility, as she quickly mastered and fell in love with sewing. 'My upbringing also taught me to appreciate living simply and to appreciate the land. I'm a lifestyler from way, way back,' she says, with a laugh.

After leaving school, Sandra trained as a sample machinist, making one-off pre-production garments for the fashion industry. Her overseas travels saw her working in the United Kingdom, Europe and Australia, gaining experience across a wide range of fashion. While in Java she attended courses in batik dyeing and silk painting, igniting her passion for handcrafted fabrics. 'I enjoyed meeting these people. They had few resources but worked with simple techniques using what they had.'

In 1998 Sandra took a felting course, leading to her dyeing her own fibres, and then purchasing her first loom in 2009. She now owns three looms. 'I learn a new technique and then I see how I can adapt it into something that I like. I don't want to copy. I want to put my own unique stamp on it.'

Sandra has an extensive list of awards and exhibitions in New Zealand and Australia, and continues to attend and run workshops on a wide range of textile-related topics. Over the years she has had to reinvent her styling in line with market trends. For a time she was a member of a co-operative art shop in Russell,

but as times changed she had to seek new ways of marketing her garments. Her work is now found all over the world. 'A highlight for me is meeting the people who buy my garments, and getting to know them as they come back for more. I think they really like the experience of being able to buy from the creator, seeing me in my workroom.' This has led Sandra to open her studio to the public through the art trails and by appointment.

Talking of the future she says, 'I'll never give up work. The word retirement is just silly. I'm so grateful to be able to live here in my paradise and create what I create. Inspiration is all around me. I don't pick up fashion magazines. I just look at the natural environment.'

Jo Dixey
Helensville

A Stitch in Time

A professional embroiderer? Are you serious? Can you actually earn a living in New Zealand from hand embroidery? Well, as I soon found out, the answer is yes, and Jo is one of only a handful of people in New Zealand doing it.

Jo is a vibrant, zany, fun-loving person who is not afraid to put her sometimes controversial ideas out there, and yet she is trained in and uses traditional hand embroidery techniques. There is something timeless about embroidery, but there is nothing timeless about Jo's messages, which are up to the minute, thought provoking and sometimes unashamedly confronting.

Jo has deliberately shunned many things other crafters put high on the list of studio must-haves, like the separate working space. Her studio opens directly into the combined family, dining, and living area. There are no doors. Everything is on show, mess and all, and although her work occasionally travels out the doorway it is easily tidied back. 'The advantage is that I can get so much done,' says Jo. 'I've got five minutes while waiting for dinner to cook so I can go and make a few more stitches.'

Growing up in England, Jo always had a passion for embroidery. As a young child she would save her pocket money for a year and blow it all at the

Knitting and Stitching Show. It was at one of these shows that Jo saw a Royal School of Needlework demonstration. Her mother was a stitcher and Jo had all the encouragement she needed to take on a three-year apprenticeship, having first done the 'sensible thing' of completing her A levels. Thinking about this brings a sparkle to Jo's eyes. 'I've never had to have a proper job. I've never needed my A level chemistry.' I can hear teenagers all around the country saying, 'See, Mum!'

Initially thinking she would like to do embroidery conservation work, Jo soon found working on old, faded and dusty embroideries was not for her. She wanted to create her own. The manager of the Royal Schools workroom recognised this also, and at the end of her three-year apprenticeship Jo's contract was not renewed. Deciding she needed more design knowledge to be successful as a freelance embroiderer, Jo embarked on a City and Guilds embroidery course, which focused on design rather than technique.

Following her partner to New Zealand brought opportunities that Jo believes she would not have got in England. The first was embroidering an altar cloth for the Rangiātea Church in Otaki. The original church had been the oldest Māori church in New Zealand and, after it was burnt down, the decision was made to rebuild it exactly as it had been — right down to remaking the original altar cloth, which Jo was given pictures of to work from. The second opportunity was to make an altar cloth for St Faith's church in Rotorua as part of a recognition package for the gallantry of Lance Sergeant Haane Manahi. Following Manahi's death in 1986 the Te Arawa people lobbied the New Zealand government to make representations to Buckingham Palace to have the Victoria Cross awarded posthumously, an award they believed he should have been given during the war. Because of the length of time elapsed, the Queen did not award the VC and opted instead for a recognition package, which included the altar cloth made by Jo, a personal letter from the Queen acknowledging his gallantry, and a sword. These were presented to Manahi's sons in 2007. Both commissions brought new challenges for Jo: the first working from a picture, and the second working with the Cabinet Office and the voluminous contract requirements they imposed. Both of these projects took around 18 months to complete. Another exciting project was to make the graduation banners for each faculty of the University of Auckland. Thinking she had finished, she delivered the banners only to find that one faculty had changed its name and another banner was urgently needed.

Jo runs workshops throughout New Zealand, mainly in gold work, silk shading (which she refers to as colouring in), and black work. She also works on her own exhibition pieces. Jo's current work is themed around cellphones and the way they impede normal interaction. The juxtaposition of traditional embroidery techniques and modern, somewhat controversial messages creates strong, confronting pieces. 'I do work that makes someone else have those conversations', says Jo. 'I need to do it, because I have something to say. I have to get it out of my system' Even the titles are confronting: *Please Turn off Your Cellphone*; *Nothing to Say*; *500 Friends but All Alone*; and *The New Face to Face* (referring to Facebook).

Jo has strong views about other things. There is no television in the house, as she prefers her children to read or play creatively. She is also passionate about making the world a better place. She's doing her bit to prevent sweat shops for clothing manufacture, by sourcing her clothing through op shops or making her own. Jo also makes dresses, for Dress a Girl Around the World (see below) and has been known to yarn bomb. 'It's something I do sometimes, I stitch bits of knitting to lamp posts or trees, just to make people smile. I've made fabric bunting and hung it up in places too,' says Jo.

'For Dress a Girl Around the World — www.dressagirlsaroundtheworld.com —

we make new dresses for girls, often the only new dress the girl will ever own. I sew on a small label that says Dress a Girl, and send them off to all sorts of places via aid workers. In countries where there are problems with child trafficking or abuse, a child with a new dress (which has a label) indicates that an organisation is looking after the girl, and that someone other than the girl's family will be checking on her wellbeing. A trafficker is less likely to buy or kidnap that child as they know the girl would be missed if whoever gave them the dress came back.'

What struck me most about Jo was how strong a work ethic she has. This is her job. She works it like a job, doing her Mum thing before seeing the kids off to school, stepping into her studio to go to work, and then coming out of the studio to do the Mum thing again when the kids arrive home from school. She is good at multi-tasking. Even a trip to the local skatepark provides ideas, which she records in sketches, photos and writing in her always carried notebook. She is super-organised with 'to do' lists and diaries, a trait that does not always sit harmoniously alongside creative flair. I found myself making a few work resolutions as I drove home after meeting her. A good example of Jo's commitment is the '100-day challenge'. How many ladies do you know that start these and don't complete 100 projects within the 100 days? Not Jo. Having spotted a golden orb spider (from Australia) in the garden, and having rung the Department of Conservation to see if she should be concerned, Jo set out to embroider 100 spiders, one each day. She is currently working on a new 100-day challenge making case moths.

Looking into the future Jo is working hard on her first book, which includes a graduated series of projects starting with very simple ones for the absolute beginner, and building skills with each successive project. Entitled *Stitch People*, it is sure to be a winner both here and overseas.

Sandra Hosking
Whenuapai

A Gift from Jess

Of all the stories here, this one most touched my heart. Having myself suffered the profoundly life-altering grief of losing a child, I immediately found a sense of connection with Sandra. I am in awe of how she has rebuilt her life and am reminded again of the healing power of creative endeavours. To Sandra, my sincere thanks for allowing me to share your very personal story.

Sandra and Mark were like many couples who were empty nesters. They had worked hard for years, bought a place at the beach, sold their house in Auckland and not yet bought another, and were imagining the next chapter in their lives. Six weeks prior, they had farewelled their only child, Jess, who was embarking on her big OE, starting by joining her paternal grandparents in London. Then tragedy struck. The couple received the call that no parent ever wants to receive. Jess, who by this time was living and working as a nanny in Paris, had passed away in her sleep the previous night. She was just three weeks short of her twentieth birthday. Mark had spoken to her the night before she died, and she had excitedly shared the plans she had for the next day. Jess had wanted to talk to Sandra, but she had not been at home. The next day Sandra returned the call. The telephone was answered by the children's grandmother, who called out for Jess, but couldn't awaken her. Unbeknown to Sandra, Jess had already passed away. Mark and Sandra would receive the news the following day from Mark's brother-in-law in England.

Because of investigations by the French authorities it wasn't until 17 days after she died that Jess's body arrived back in New Zealand. Sandra could tell me the exact dates without even thinking about it.

Jess's funeral service was held at the stadium at the Waitemata rugby ground, which had been decorated by her friends in the style of Taylor Swift's music video, *Mine*. Hundreds of photos had been strung from the rafters, and friends and family were invited to take one of the photos with them as a keepsake.

Sandra describes Jess as fun loving and optimistic. 'She had so much energy. She hated to sit still.' Jess was also a creative person, studying visual art and design at Unitec. Incredibly outgoing, she would do anything for anybody, loved a party, and believed a smile could solve any problem.

This is, however, Sandra's story. Like any bereaved parent, they will tell you that to understand them, you need to understand the tragedy that has changed their lives.

A short time after Jess's passing, Sandra had a serious fall at the Rugby World Cup at Eden Park, aggravating a previous back injury. She spent three weeks in the November after Jess's funeral in hospital. At a time when she most needed to stay busy Sandra was laid up with nothing but time on her hands to think. Sandra had to give up full-time work and still experiences pain on a daily basis. She has no feeling in her lower leg and is very careful about how long she sits, and how she engages in even the simplest of physical activity, such as walking or bending.

You will recall from above that Mark and Sandra had sold their house just before Jess died, in fact only one week before she passed away. After much looking they purchased a house not far from the old one, moving from a 250 square metre house to a 60 square metre house. The considerable downsizing no doubt added to the stress of the move, with those all too difficult decisions about what to keep.

In pride of place on the lounge wall is a painting by 12-year-old Jess and a friend. It cost her parents $500 at a school fundraiser. There's also a photo taken by Jess at age 13, and inspirational words, which Jess had started to paint and which Sandra has finished off.

It is in the corner of the combined kitchen/lounge space of their new home that Sandra started what was to become her new love, making costume

jewellery. Her workspace measures two by three metres. This space includes Sandra's work desk and numerous storage drawers and cupboards.

Jess had left behind a number of boxes of jewellery pieces when she left for London and, with nothing else to do, Sandra started putting together necklaces, bracelets and earrings from these pieces. As Jess's friends started to turn 21, Sandra made jewellery for them. 'It was like giving a gift from Jess,' she says. Encouraged by friends and family Sandra made more and slowly her business — MSJ Jewellery (M for Mark, S for Sandra, J for Jess) — was started. When she was able to move around more easily she started attending local markets, but found it difficult to compete with cheap imported jewellery. Like all good business people, Sandra was not deterred and approached Craftworld at Auckland's Westgate shopping centre. Initially sales were slow but when December came, sales lifted and have continued to grow from then on.

As Sandra became better known she began to get requests for made-to-order jewellery. One recommendation landed her the job of working with a woman who wanted a necklace and earrings to wear on her wedding day — made from a necklace that had belonged to her mother. Speaking about her bespoke work, Sandra says, 'I do a lot of consultation, getting to know them

[the client] and choosing the main pieces they like. Then I ask them to trust me to build the rest.'

Every piece she makes is different, and while she can make something similar, she will never make two pieces that are exactly the same. Her range includes 'bread and butter' lines like her angel and skull bracelets, which are her most popular, through to more expensive pieces such as Swarovski crystal bracelets and necklaces. 'It's about learning your market,' she says. 'I've learnt a lot about merchandising.' It was listening to her market that led Sandra to do jewellery repair work and expand into beaded Christmas decorations.

Sandra works on her jewellery range around eight hours a week. She has also returned to her job at Unitec for 15 hours a week, where she supports the Bachelor of Social Practice fieldwork team, and she continues her role on the board of the Piha Surf Life Saving Club, where she was the first woman board member since the club's inception over 80 years ago. Despite numerous setbacks in her journey, she is positive and upbeat about the future.

Vanessa York
Waiake, Auckland

Fleurs du Mal — 'Flowers of Evil'?

There's something romantic about perfume, with its sense of occasion, glamour and beautiful alluring scents, and the idea of a natural, artisan perfume has a particularly special charm. For many people, perfume making is not something particularly associated with New Zealand, but there are a growing number of local perfumers who are proving that beautiful perfumes are not just the domain of the French. Vanessa York is one of those artisan perfumers.

A couple of years ago Vanessa left her publishing industry job of 15 years. Having always had an interest in natural skincare and French perfume (like many women, hers had to be French), Vanessa started experimenting with essential oils. Searching for more information, she joined internet forums and discovered the natural perfumery movement. 'This really appealed to me,' she says. 'Simple and beautiful.'

Vanessa began blending essential oils in a corner of an upstairs bedroom, gradually accumulating a collection of aromatics. There is a sense of mystery around perfume making just as there is around winemaking, and Vanessa

sees many parallels between the two industries: the French connection, and the effect of the environment on the quality of the raw materials. Adding to the sense of mystery is the musical language used to describe perfumes. Perfumers talk about base notes, top notes, chords and a perfume organ. 'The top note evaporates first, and is the first fragrance we smell,' she explains. 'I start with an idea. It could be a word or a name, and I ask myself how would that work as a perfume? Starting with two elements, I test out different ratios until I am happy with the balance, or group of notes, known as a chord. Once I'm happy with a blend the perfume then has to be aged for a few months as it goes on changing in the bottle.' The blending takes place at the perfume organ, traditionally an organ-shaped desk with shelves full of aromatics. 'What's lovely about working with naturals is they are forever changing. The oil from one season to the next may be different, and oils grown in one region will differ from those grown in another region. You are constantly learning.'

Vanessa credits the internet with making it easier to get information and supplies, most of which come from overseas, particularly from Australia and the United States. She studied with the Natural Perfumery Institute in Florida, learning the classical traditions, the structure, the science, and how to weigh proportions and balance perfumes. 'As a researcher, I was used to seeking out information, but you have to be careful: not knowing something can undermine your confidence. There is a saying I like, "Try not to be intimidated by what you don't know". I'm not very methodical or scientific about it. I try things. Most times they work, but sometimes they don't,' she says.

Vanessa quickly outgrew her bedroom corner and has now moved into a large, spacious room downstairs, which smells absolutely delicious. She treats her passion as her day job: going downstairs each morning and working in the space at whatever needs to be done. 'Success is about showing up. You have to be there in the space,' she says. 'I need time just messing around. This is my space. My family respect my time when I'm down here. They ask permission to come in, rather than just barging in.'

Vanessa's favourite item in her perfumery is, naturally, her perfume organ. It's an old, solid, wooden desk, which she found on the side of the road right around the time she decided to make the perfumery her full-time business. There's a packing table and shelves of aging and bottled perfumes, and an array of beakers, test tubes, scales and droppers, which add to the visual experience. 'I like my beakers and test tubes,' says Vanessa. 'Perfume making is a very tactile experience.'

Vanessa's business and perfume label is Fleurs du Mal, which translates to flowers of evil. The name comes from a book by French poet Charles Baudelaire, which was published in 1857 and was notorious for celebrating things not ordinarily written about in poetry — sex, death, urban corruption and loss of innocence to name but a few. It was both a great scandal and a great success. 'I don't want to focus on just the happy and the good,' says Vanessa. 'Life isn't like that. I make spiky perfumes that not all people will like. Natural perfumes also react differently on the skin, and get more personal in comparison to synthetic or mixed perfumes. I like green perfumes with earthy base tones: blends of oak moss and patchouli, and my favourite, called Violet Moss, made with violet leaf and galbanum. Blending them is an art.'

Vanessa has big dreams for the future. She is keen to see her artisan business grow into a flourishing perfumery, and for New Zealand to gain a reputation for excellent perfumes just as it has for wine. At present, the industry is focused on lavender and New Zealand natives such as manuka, but with the growing number of aromatics available worldwide, particularly new ones which are viable now due to improved technology, there is huge scope for industry growth.

Along with a flourishing perfumery business, she sees a beautiful facility, separate from the house, which includes a space for teaching. Vanessa's workshops in perfume making are oversubscribed, a testament to the growing interest in natural perfumes. She has plans to run a specific New Zealand perfumery workshop. 'What does New Zealand smell like?' she asks. 'There is nothing more satisfying than getting people passionate about your passion.' Included in the plans is an ongoing investment in self-development. Vanessa is currently studying business management. She believes this will assist her in growing her business in a sustainable way, planning and balancing production, and marketing her product. Vanessa currently sells directly through her website and the Auckland Fair, and is also planning a retail range. 'I love markets, though,' she says. 'You get so much feedback,' she laughs as she describes how she has had to learn to accept praise. 'I wonder if they're just being nice to me. If I had more money would I feel more legitimate? But I'm immensely proud of what I have achieved. It's all part of the learning curve, and about building self-belief.' I wonder why so many of us find praise difficult to accept.

Dagmar Dyck

Mt Wellington, Auckland

With Thanks to My Teacher

Dagmar Dyck has an impressive CV that any artist would aspire to. She has an extensive list of both solo and group exhibitions in New Zealand and overseas, and has been the recipient of many awards. But things could have been quite different had it not been for the actions of her third-form art teacher, renowned New Zealand artist Judy Darragh, who told a careers counsellor to make sure Dagmar carried on with her art. 'I was about to drop art as I couldn't see how it could add value to my future. Luckily Judy saw things differently. It just shows how the influence of a teacher can be critical,' Dagmar says. And she should know as she is now a specialist art teacher at Sylvia Park Primary School.

Much of the motivation for Dagmar's printmaking and painting practice is closely aligned with her Tongan, German, Dutch and Polish ancestry. As first-generation New Zealanders growing up during the mid-eighties on Auckland's North Shore, Dagmar and her sister were among only a handful of Pasifika students at their secondary school and were often assumed to be Māori. Through the encouragement of Dagmar's teachers, art became a vehicle for exploring her cultural identity and telling her story. 'Being in the art room felt natural, and a safe place to express myself,' she says.

Attending Elam School of Fine Arts, Dagmar settled on a print major in order to learn the technical processes associated with that medium. Art school allowed Dagmar time and space to explore and experiment with multiple print processes, finally settling on her preferred methods of screen and woodcut.

Over the last 20 years, Dagmar has created a large body of work that delves beneath the decorative surfaces of Tongan koloa, material wealth, produced predominantly by Tongan women. Koloa includes the production of ngatu (bark cloths), fala (mats), ta'ovala (waist mats), kiekie (waist garments), and kato alu (baskets).

Dagmar's early works with her unique hybrid iconography reflect her inner motivation to seek a connection to her taonga.

Over the years, Dagmar has made sacrifices in balancing her many roles as professional artist, full-time teacher, wife and mother. She made the decision to take six years out of the art scene to devote time to raising her pre-school children, a period of time she reflects as small in the overall scheme of things, yet still difficult at the time. 'It was the best decision I made; the children's pre-school years are beautiful memories that I treasure. As a result the children, alongside my husband, all respect my art career and, of course, I deeply value their support.'

Dagmar is a prolific artist, with a large volume of both print works on paper and paintings. She describes her studio in her garage as her sanctuary. 'I deliberately surround myself with things that are important to me.'

The studio is full of materials, research images, memories, treasures, quotes, and books — including many years' worth of visual diaries. There's lots of colour from plastic leis, a treasured Princess Diana tin, and a favourite quote from Australian abstract painter, Ann Thomson: 'Creating something is more letting go than thinking.'

'I've grown to appreciate it [the studio] as my life gathers momentum. My space is a visual reminder to my family that my art making is an intrinsic part of me.' But while the space is important, you get the feeling that Dagmar could create anywhere. She carries it with her wherever she goes.

Dagmar prefers working towards a body of work. On the walls are photos of woven mats she is using as inspiration for her current exhibition. The easel is covered in two-metre-long strips of four-strand plaiting, which started life as paper she has printed on both sides. She has plans for a big wallpaper installation.

At her school, Dagmar's work is also very evident. Her classroom is an engaging place where students are free to express themselves visually. 'I count it a real privilege to empower the next generation of creatives. I work hard to provide an environment that is safe yet encourages risk-taking, where the individual voice and mark is respected and most importantly valued,' she says.

Dagmar recalls significant milestones: her careers counsellor meeting; being the first woman of Tongan descent to graduate from Elam; her sell-out first solo exhibition at age 23; attending exhibitions in China, Norway, Germany and Tahiti; and attending the King of Tonga's coronation in 2015. Her work hangs in New Zealand trade and consular offices in Tonga, Hong Kong and South America and is also a part of the New Zealand parliamentary art collection. It can also be found in a number of government ministry offices, city council offices, universities, schools and hotels.

Dagmar says: 'Over the course of my career I've often been fortunate to be in the right place at the right time. I have learnt to seize opportunities and understand that good things take time. Failures are inevitable but ultimately help shape your character. Thankfully, an artist's career does not have an expiry date so I know that I still have the best years ahead of me. That thought alone keeps my creative juices flowing.'

Julie Jensen
Tuateawa, Coromandel

Letting the Madness Out

What do bikes, chairs, vegetables, flowers, burley bags, cacti, garden gates and knitting wool have in common? The answer is Julie Jensen, knitter, crafter and recycler extraordinaire — and yes, she has knitted all of the above!

I first came across Julie's extraordinary work in Whitianga gallery Mosaic, when the owner Morag said, 'You've got to come and look at this. I thought of you the moment I saw it.' She took me into her office and showed me an old government department chair that was now covered in knitting. Lynn of Tawa would have quite rightly described it as 'a visual symphony'. In another Whitianga shop, Mrs Smith's, not only was there another amazing chair but also a bicycle completely covered in knitting, with knitted handlebars, sprockets, pedals and chain. The only parts that weren't knitted were the spokes! It was festooned with an array of knitted flowers and added birds. It was a real eye-catcher.

When I went to visit Julie, I was more than a little curious as to who I would be meeting. Julie is an upbeat lady with a vivid and comedic imagination. Her two great loves are crafting and gardening. Having spent years working in an

office in Hamilton, Julie and her builder husband decided they were over it and retreated to their 1.2 hectare Coromandel paradise, just north of Kennedy Bay. At the time Julie told her husband, 'I'm going to let the madness out.' He immediately replied, 'I thought you already had!'

Madness it might be, but what has resulted is a spectacular garden. Every corner of it reflects Julie's 'craftiness' and imagination, and the hub for all this activity is her outdoor craft room known as her 'imaginarium'. Originally a sleep-out — it still has the bed in it, which family members love to sleep in — this homely space houses Julie's craft supplies and more than a few treasures, including an old Robertson sewing machine that used to belong to Julie's grandmother, and her father's photo album documenting his world travels as an engineer with the merchant navy.

Julie doesn't like to throw anything away. Finding old silverware whose plating had worn away, she made a series of chalkboard platters as gifts. She loves the challenge of giving new life to something others would throw out, and that's how she got started knitting, well, everything — from chairs, to bikes, to chandeliers. 'I think I have a chair fixation,' Julie says. 'I have a million chairs in my head.'

As a young mum, Julie knitted for her family, but as hand-knitted garments eventually lost the fashion race, she turned to other things. Her first chair was made as a display chair for a friend who runs an Otorohanga opportunity

shop. This was followed by others: a vegetable stool featuring rows of knitted cabbages and cauliflowers; and a ladder-back chair with a cat chasing a mouse up the leg. Her quirky chairs have earned her a reputation, with family, friends and acquaintances now sourcing 'no longer loved chairs' for Julie from all over the country.

Julie treated me to a walk around her spectacular garden, which is divided into a series of rooms each with a special focal point. There are pathways and hidden gardens and garden art, making the tour a real adventure. An inflatable swimming pool for the grandchildren sits atop a set of mosaic stairs, which are the entranceway to a private courtyard. In another courtyard is an outdoor bath complete with hot running water.

The planting is particularly lush, with an abundance of nīkau palms and hydrangeas, many of which have been grown from cuttings raised in Julie's glasshouse. 'Gardening here is challenging,' explains Julie. 'The earth is solid

clay and rock, with little topsoil, that becomes puggy in winter and dries out in the summer due to the wind, and we can't water anything because we rely on rainwater supplies.'

There were so many favourite pieces as I walked around the garden: the life-sized doll sitting in the hedge that had been Julie's contribution to a Christmas parade float, the mosaic obelisks, and a knitted gate, made from baling twine.

Julie clearly likes to stay busy. 'I can do two hours of gardening, and then I have to park myself. Yes, there will be lots more knitting.' But I'm really curious to know what Julie will do with the set of piano keys mounted on the garage wall. 'I'm still working on that one,' she says.

Bev Johnstone
Coromandel Town

A World in Miniature

On the Whangapoua Road, just out of Coromandel, tucked down a right-of-way is a 1.2 hectare section complete with sheep paddock and native bush and a world in miniature called 'Over the Fence'. It is home to Bev Johnstone and her extensive collection of handcrafted miniature doll's houses, farms and imaginary worlds.

There is a two-storey house, home to the Seven Dwarfs, complete with a diamond mine below. Yes, there are seven beds, seven chairs, a table with food on it, and miniature lights on the walls. The detail is incredible. For the younger children there are nursery rhymes and storybook characters, each in their own settings: the Old Woman Who Lived in a Shoe, Hansel and Gretel, Three Little Pigs, Jack and the Beanstalk . . . such wonderful reminders of childhood memories.

When I asked Bev how this all got started she replied, 'I always wanted a doll's house when I was little, so I made one from two wooden apple boxes and some tiny plastic furniture.' It wasn't until Bev retired that she had the time to indulge her passion again. Bev took out a subscription for *Doll's House Step-by-Step* magazine, with each issue providing the pieces to build a doll's house and furniture. She started creating the furniture first, as it was easy to do while looking after her grandchild and her elderly father-in-law. From there she just started collecting 'stuff' and her collection grew until it took over the garage and the spare bedroom. She laughs as she tells me she still hasn't made up the house from the magazine.

One of the first doll's houses Bev created — now named the *Artist's House* — was a kitset one that was intended for children. Not satisfied with its painted cardboard appearance Bev sought out a collection of bread tags she had stored in the garage. She then set about individually cutting hundreds of tags to make roof tiles, which she then painted. With similar ingenuity she covered the Seven Dwarfs' house in slivers of road metal from the local quarry, and she sheathed the base and stand in gum bark, which she collected from a tree down the road.

When creating the miniature worlds, Bev makes up stories about the characters. 'I want to put the heart and soul into each display,' she says. To enhance the story, each house is placed in surroundings: the lake house sits beside a mirror lake with a mountainous backdrop; the witches' coven is in the brick fireplace complete with mantel and fire surround. Using specialty containers Bev has created a bakehouse scene inside a Cookie Time jar, and — my favourite — the dressmaker's shop made in a vintage suitcase complete with miniature cotton reels, stacks of fabric and a dressmaker's dummy. But it's not all girly stuff either. There's a military base complete with action figures and jeeps, and a farmyard complete with house, barn and paddocks with animals.

Bev sees the potential in everything. She loves searching out bits and pieces at garage sales and second-hand shops, and has amassed a collection of antique china, including a large number of doll's tea sets. 'I see things and think I could do something with that,' like her recent acquisitions, miniature leather jackets, from key rings, which will become part of a character's

clothing. 'Probably a rock star,' she says. She even has a miniature drum kit for him to sit at, and is eyeing up a glass shelf from a DVD cabinet that could work as a stage.

Another house is being created in an old grandfather clock she rescued from a bonfire. It will find a new lease of life as a multi-storey bordello, complete with reception area, lounges, bedrooms and the madam's office on the top floor. One small item can spark a whole story in her head. 'They're like my babies — but these ones will never grow up. I always have several projects on the go at once. You have to wait for glue to set or paint to dry.'

About two-and-a-half years ago — having grown out of the garage and bedroom — Bev bought a prefab building from the local school. She and her husband, Mocky, spent the next few months doing it up. Once the decorating was complete, she began to assemble her display, which takes up the entire prefab except for one small corner where she makes her creations. Bev's workspace is incredibly organised with labelled drawers and boxes, paints and finished pieces.

Her future plans include building a carport off the back of the prefab that she can use to house outdoor scenes. 'I want to build a hill and create bush shanties and old baches, stepping back through the years. I could have a stone church and a general store, and a waterfall and a river,' she says, her happiness and enthusiasm brimming over.

Bev now opens her 'Over the Fence' display to the public. It is well worth the visit, but check out the dates and times as they vary throughout the year. There is something for all ages and it's bound to put a smile on your face.

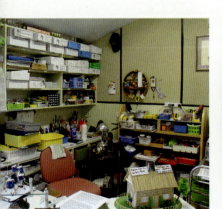

Christine Sedgwick
Whitianga

Memorable Moments

Like many crafty women, Christine's earliest recollections of making things are of her grandmothers who were never without a piece of needlework. They created in Christine a love of all things hand-stitched, from felting, to knitting, to embroidery.

Christine definitely has the magpie thing happening. Everywhere you look in her comfortable and homely two-bedroom unit, there are bits and pieces, work in progress, and finished work. Whether sitting on the couch looking at the view over Mercury Bay, or fossicking through her remarkably tidy and organised drawers of fabric, Christine always has inspiration at hand.

Christine keeps the majority of her fabrics, beads, threads and embellishments in her spare bedroom. One wall is lined with tallboys and bookshelves, each drawer brimming with trims awaiting Christine's creative eye. The walls and the bed display a number of Christine's craftwork pieces. There are beaded Christmas stockings and a cane basket containing Christine's latest crochet project — a blanket in soft mauve shades. On the tallboy are samples of her whimsical knitted caps for boiled eggs and her small knitted animals. There's a knitted handbag and a beaded velvet clutch purse. The range of creations is quite extraordinary, demonstrating Christine's versatility as a crafter.

But the place where you are most likely to find Christine is sitting in the corner of the lounge working on her current crafting projects. Around her is a fascinating range of embroidery threads in every colour of the rainbow, and pieces of tatting and small silk flowers. Unlike some artists, who choose to have a separate dedicated space for their activity, Christine likes to have everything around her. 'I can do what I like, when I like, where I like.'

Many of the bits and pieces have been given to her. 'People know what I do and they just give me things. It doesn't matter what it is. If I look at it for long enough I can always find something to do with it.'

An example of Christine's thoughtful repurposing can be seen in the oversize cotton reels that now form the bases of her folk-art pincushions. Christine has made a huge number of these over the years, finding them extremely popular in shops. Every one of them is different; some are made of felt, some from wool. There is a range of sizes and each has a different theme and set of embellishments — flowers, leaves, or birds.

Christine's first project was an Edwardian cushion made while attending a class in Devonport in 1997. Being a traditional embroidery course, the stitching requirements were exacting. It was here Christine experienced her first frustration of going to courses. 'They want you to do it their way, but I want to do it my way, and put my own twist on it.' That hasn't deterred her though, as Christine has attended a number of courses over the years to gain the basic skills, which she then goes on to use in her own unique way.

Christine is always experimenting with different techniques and materials and enjoys the challenges each new medium brings. A few years ago she experimented with mosaics, creating two-dimensional pictures and sculptures. She was commissioned by Oceania Healthcare to create a piece entitled *Three Nikaus* for their reception area in their Whitianga care facility. There are other examples of her work on display in her living room, including a very special piece, entitled *Mother's Conception*, inspired by her niece's first pregnancy. It features a women's torso wrapped in a feather cloak, with the body made in pāua mosaic, including a foetus depicted as a koru. For Christine, it is a very spiritual piece. Also special to her is a felted table runner in rustic tan, cream and olive colours.

I met Christine at the beginning of August and she was already under way with her first orders for hand-stitched Christmas decorations — beaded hearts, bells and Christmas stockings. They are simply exquisite, with such attention to detail, each one different from the next. Christine supplies local art and craft shops, but is also building up a loyal clientele who place repeat orders each year. Her ultimate goal is to be able to give up her night-shift nursing job, and go full-time into crafting.

Dhyana Muir & Reina Cottier

Tairua, Coromandel

Soul Sisters

While shopping in a Thames bookshop I came across a book called *The Dreamcatcher*. The cover caught my eye and I was delighted to find it was a local book created by merging the talents of two Tairua artists. The combination of the Pasifika-styled artwork of Reina, the photography of Dhyana, and the spiritual nature of the storyline is truly unique, and I was captivated by the richness of the colours and the powerful imagery. The book, the first of a series, features a mythical Pasifika woman, *The Dreamcatcher*, who interprets children's dreams, bringing them positive messages and encouragement.

Dhyana and Reina have been friends for over 42 years, describing themselves as soul sisters. They met at an Auckland ballet class at age seven. 'Our eyes met across the room, and we both recognised an instant connection,' says Dhyana.

Growing up, they spent a considerable amount of time at each other's houses, and although they did not attend the same schools, their friendship

flourished throughout their school years and has continued throughout their adult lives. It is clear there is a deep connection and understanding between them.

Dhyana and Reina both came from creative homes. Reina's parents were actors, and her mother was wardrobe mistress for a number of shows. Costumes and props frequently took over the space and their lives as show deadlines loomed. It was chaotic and sometimes pressurised, but it was fun. To Dhyana, Reina's home allowed her to feel free, fostering her artistic expression. Dhyana's home was also creative, but in a different way. 'My mother is incredibly creative, skilled in many crafts including knitting, sewing, and home decorating.'

Dhyana (above left) picked up the camera at an early age. A career in fashion and modelling led to the development of a children's fashion line and ultimately to portfolio shoots for actors and models. She started photographing nature and patterns developing a range of greeting cards, and later merged these two styles of photography to create her own unique style of layered photographs.

Alongside her developing creativity Dhyana took up yoga, which she has taught for the last 18 years. It was through yoga that Dhyana was introduced to the meditation techniques that led her to develop the concept and storyline for the book series.

About five years ago Dhyana moved to Tairua, to get away from the hustle and bustle of Auckland, and to further her creative expression. While working in an art gallery in Tairua she recalled a mentor asking her some years ago, 'When are you going to put down that camera and be the artist you are?' Following a car accident, Dhyana did exactly that and started painting prolifically. Her studio (page 52, top) is a light-filled space, with wall-to-wall paintings, and a large worktable in the centre. Dhyana's work is varied: there are large abstract canvases, paintings on glass, and photographs. Speaking of her space she says, 'It is a haven for

writing, painting and planning my creativity/ yoga retreats. I like to have everything out around me. It's important not to have to put things away,' she says. 'This is a place to experiment and remember how far I've come and where I am going.'

On leaving school Reina (middle left) became a hairdresser, owning her own salon. 'Creatively, it was excellent,' says Reina, 'but when my life became too "businessy" I needed to get out.' After selling the salon and starting a family, she began searching for a new creative outlet. Reina's artistic journey received a kick-start when she attended a course called 'Awaken the Artist Within'. 'I learnt so much about creative approach and letting go.'

Reina began painting for her personal pleasure, then for friends and before long she was selling her work. She worked on developing her own unique style — large acrylic paintings, which resonate with tribal and spiritual influences. Speaking of her first studio in her garage she says, 'I was very protective of my space. I didn't want the kids in there.'

Not long after Dhyana moved to Tairua, Reina and her family followed, making a home through the summer in her tiny family bach and caravan, and later renting in the cold winter months. 'I have so many memories here. I've been coming here since I was seventeen. I feel the history and the energy of those wonderful times in the garage.' The garage was converted into her studio, and

Reina has made the most of the space (page 52, bottom), with display shelves for her cards, calendars and colouring books. There's a large table for packing her paintings, which she freights around the world, with her work now residing in Australia, Canada, England, Switzerland, Germany, the United States, Holland, Italy, France, Mexico and Brazil.

In just the right space, with light from four directions, and a sea breeze coming in, is her easel. The seat is, of course, a hairdressing stool. Everything is at arm's reach. 'It's a sensual experience,' she says, speaking of her painting. 'I become a channel for whatever comes through in the moment. I don't plan my paintings. I create the background and by the time that's finished I know what I want to do. I build the picture up in layers, leaving the intricate details until the last layer. I love the motifs of the Pasifika, Native American and Asian cultures. I often have six canvases on the go at once, so I can allow drying time, and time for my vision to develop.'

Reina's artwork has a spiritual quality to it, almost as though she has captured the spirituality of her artistic process on the canvas. The ethereal images, with their hint of the unknown, draw you into the depths of the painting, and the meaning that lies beyond.

Over the years Reina has been committed to the business side of her artwork, investing an hour a day to promoting her work online, something she says has really paid off. 'Ninety-nine per cent of my work is sold through Facebook.'

The online nature of her business meant that her customers were completely unaware of her change of address. 'Moving to Tairua has brought new opportunities. Through exhibitions and the Art Trail I've had the chance to interact face to face with people interested in my work. I'm enjoying that.'

Talking of the future, Reina excitedly reveals her plans to move house: 'Getting a bigger studio and house space is very important, as well as spending time with my family. I want to be a shining beacon; an example to my children. Having balance in life is extremely important. If I'm not happy, how can I raise happy kids?' she says. 'Art is not the number one priority, but it's pretty close to the top.'

Getting Started Creatively

> *Start where you are.
> Use what you have.
> Do what you can.*
>
> — Arthur Ashe

If you are at the beginning of your creative journey or yearning to recapture creativity from the past, then this section is for you.

Many of the women interviewed for this book talked about having to get past their own personal expectations or those of family or friends. 'I should have a job, I should save the money for something more important, I should have a tidy house. I should . . . I should . . . I should . . .' Whatever your 'should' is, take the pressure off yourself and give yourself permission to be creative for no other reason than being creative. Who knows where it could lead.

There will never be a perfect time. Now is as perfect as it can get. Life will always find a reason for you not to get started and there will always be something on the 'to do' list. Plan and prioritise creative time for yourself each week. Two hours is a good goal, preferably in a large chunk rather than doing 20 minutes a day.

Don't wait for the perfect space. Many of the women I met started their creative journeys at the kitchen table and some are still at the kitchen table. Look for solutions. If you really don't have space at home, talk to friends or family. Someone is bound to have a corner you can get started in.

Use what you have. Chances are you already have a collection of paints and brushes, fabrics and trims, or whatever it is you need to get started. If you haven't and money is tight, make things out of junk. Recycle, restore and repurpose. You'll be right on trend. Let people know what you are doing and their junk will become your treasure. Lots of the women featured here talked about being gifted precious bits and pieces. People would far rather give things to someone than throw them away, so don't be afraid to ask. You'll be doing them a favour. If you do need new materials, and haven't got the cash, get to know the retailer. Maybe you can work for free in exchange for whatever you need. Don't let pride stop you asking.

Surround yourself with inspiration — read books, collect pictures, surf the net, pin up quotes, display special memorabilia. Create a place to store your ideas, buy a sketchbook, or open a Pinterest account. Keep the ideas flowing in and keep looking at them. Make them an active part of your week. Take time out to dream and get excited.

Build yourself a support network. Go to a course, join a group, chat on Facebook, and follow blogs. They'll be a source of inspiration and a 'go to' for information when you hit your first knowledge gap, which you will; just don't let that stop you. Don't be afraid to ask for help.

Let go of perfection. Creative work rarely goes 100 per cent according to plan. The serendipitous nature of creating is part of the process, and something which creatives grow to enjoy. Don't be afraid to take risks and experiment. The worse that could happen is that you throw something away. It's never a failure, it's something you have learnt not to do. Learning from mistakes makes good sense.

Make a mess. Creativity rarely happens in a neat and tidy way. If you can, leave things out until you're finished with them. If you have to pack up mid-stream, have a large box and put everything away together so you can quickly retrieve it.

Don't know what you want to create? Try something anyway. Either it will grab your attention or you can cross it off your list and move on to the next thing. Many of the ladies in this book tried other activities before finding their passion, but none of them spoke of those activities as a waste of time. Value each of the experiences as a learning experience, and part of your journey towards your creative passion.

Feeling creatively blocked? Try a brain dump. Either writing it down or capturing it as a sound track — record your stream-of-consciousness thinking. Just write or record whatever comes into your head. Often we get blocked because our brains are too cluttered. Brain dumping clears the mind. You may need to do this daily for a couple of weeks before you see the benefit, but it is incredibly liberating.

Start small. You may find starting with a small project less daunting. It will also give you quick satisfaction, which will spur you on to other things.

Focus on the process. Be in the moment and enjoy the journey. Let the destination — and the final product — take care of itself.

Believe that you are worth investing in creatively. You deserve to take time out. Creativity is good for your health, and if you are anything like the women in this book, you will be a better person for taking time out to be creative. So what are you waiting for?

Gin Clay
Kopu, Thames

Baroness Ditzy von Karbon

Tucked down a right-of-way off the Kopu-Hikuai road, hidden amongst the trees on 26 hectares of bush, with a stream gurgling and cicadas singing, is the delightful home and studio of Gin Clay. It is different from anything I've seen before, and I have to say Gin fits that description too — in a totally good way — because she is a steampunker. Yes, she's one of these people who dresses up in Victorian-type clothes, complete with gadget-adorned hat, corset, boots, spats and riding crop. 'You may call me Baroness Ditzy von Karbon,' she laughs. 'I'm a scientist, and a botanist, and I'm very fond of explosions!'

Creating steampunk costumes is Gin's passion and her specialties are hats, guns and accessories. Gin has a flair for collecting and arranging things for display. In fact, her workroom features a series of collections, arranged to inspire. There's a table of small metal objects, many of which have come from watches, awaiting Gin's inspiration to be repurposed into a steampunk accessory or adornment. Then there's the hat table and shelf where multiple black top hats sit expectantly awaiting their punking. There is a multitude of feathers and — a little more than I can cope with — a mummified rat and tiny mouse all ready to be included in her latest designs.

With steampunk, anything goes, and that was the message Gin and her friend Linda Stephenson (see page 61) were out to spread when they opened their pop-up shop selling steampunk costumes in Grahamstown. 'There's no wrong,' says Gin. 'If you feel like you're in the part, you're grand. A hat and boots and you're away.'

Gin works with recycled 'stuff', as she calls it. A lampshade, a rag rug, random brass and copper bits that she has collected together to make a gun, and whatever catches her eye. 'We wanted to be reasonably priced. We didn't want to make it hard for people. We wanted people to be excited by things, including what they had at home. On opening night we decided not to sell anything but just to allow people to have fun trying things on and creating their unique look. We wanted our people in Thames to be the best dressed they could be. We had such a laugh.'

Gin's creative journey started as a young child making shoebox doll's houses and fairy rings at the bottom of the garden. She says she wasn't good at school. She's tried her hand at silversmithing, ceramics, and painting and, unsurprisingly given her clear love of anything theatrical, she has also had her 'time in lights' on the stage.

Gin's house and studio combine to create her own private gallery. 'I know all the artists,' she says of the paintings on the walls. 'I know their stories and how the work came to be. I like that.'

We are sitting in the lounge area, which has a high vaulted ceiling, making it feel surprisingly spacious. The whole place oozes creativity and has a warm and welcoming feel to it. At the back is a mezzanine bedroom, with the studio tucked beneath, behind a half wall. The studio looks self-contained, but Gin assures me her creativity frequently escapes into the living area and crowds onto the leather-covered kitchen table. 'It's great. I can walk around and around

until things come together. You can't fail at this,' she says. 'Sometimes it just turns out differently and that's okay.'

Gin hasn't always lived in this house, which is a relatively recent addition to the property. Up until three years ago Gin lived in 'the cave', a hobbit-like dwelling built into the rock face. 'The cave was comfy and cosy. I was well sorted,' she says. It's an amazing space with a lounge area complete with floor rug, settee and fireplace, a kitchen and dining nook, and a bedroom space adorned with a double bed. Like the house, the cave is completely off the grid, and I can't help but imagine warm nights snuggled up by a cheery fire with a good hot toddy in your hand.

Some may call Gin a little eccentric but she loves the freedom of being and doing exactly what she pleases. 'Being older has made me bolder and braver. I don't care what people think. I'm hugely unimportant,' she says, quoting Oscar Wilde's *A Woman of No Importance*.

Gin is a fabulous storyteller and her flair for the theatrical has me in stitches. She describes past jobs such as making 'rude' cakes — moulding icing sugar and marzipan to create body parts — being a telephone clairvoyant, running a newspaper, the *Barrier Bulletin* from Waiheke Island where she lived, and managing Mama Gin's, a bar in Thames she bought on a whim with no experience at all. 'How hard can it be?' she says. I think that could be her motto for life. Nothing fazes her and everything is up for grabs — the more bizarre and hilarious, the better. With Gin, more is definitely more!

Linda Stephenson
Thames

Lady Lavinia Laudanum-Swoon

The second part of the Thames steampunk ladies duo is Linda Stephenson, a seamstress extraordinaire. Linda's passion for upcycling clothing goes back to the days of Auckland's Cook Street market, where she used to buy clothing and sell her restyled garments. Linda's creations are delightful. There's a touch of glamour in a cream and black jacket, a hint of the whimsical in a black jacket with lace bustle, and a blatant raunchiness in her satin corsets. Each garment is individually styled, a one-off, and there are racks of them, including a slinky little black Deco dress that's sure to be a winner at Napier's Art Deco Festival.

Following her early market days, Linda opened a 'his-and-hers' vintage shop called Two Timing in Canterbury Arcade, just off Auckland's Queen Street. She and her partner travelled to the United States and brought back vintage pieces to sell in the shop. When motherhood arrived, Linda closed the shop, but it wasn't long before she was back into the markets. 'Maybe I was a seamstress in a previous life,' she says. 'I just love it. I'd go to Victoria Street market, Aotea Square and Takapuna markets buying and selling.' All of which is a far cry from her original career choice of veterinary nursing.

Following her husband's work, Linda initially wasn't keen to move to Thames, but she now says it was the best move of her life. Linda continued her passion for making Art Deco clothes. 'But somewhere along the line I got hijacked by the steampunk thing,' she says. 'Even before I knew what steampunk was I loved the Victorian aesthetic, the dresses and the jewellery. I love the drama and the theatrics.

'As a child, I loved going to ballet and dressing up in tutus, and we always had dress-ups passed on to us by an auntie. As I got older I started op-shopping, something that was considered a bit of a no-no at the time. But by the eighties op-shopping had become acceptable, even fashionable. I had a black beaded tea dress with sequins. I wore it everywhere. I wanted to look like Stevie Nicks.'

Linda lives in a lovely, old, lemon-painted villa. To get to her studio you go across the back veranda, into the garden and past the original miner's cottage. 'The miner's cottage was the reason we [Linda and her husband] bought the house,' she says. They've made the cottage weather-tight inside, but left the outside original. It is both a functional and beautiful garden ornament. Behind the miner's cottage is the double garage that serves as Linda's workroom. She warned me several times that it was messy and full of 'stuff', but I could see immediately it was a creative haven for Linda. There were gorgeous lace dresses, jackets, hats and boots, all awaiting Linda's magic touch. 'I build on existing garments and embellish them,' she says. 'I don't always feel like it. My creative process ebbs and flows, but then I come in here and start putting things together and I'm away.'

Her garments are exquisitely made and would rival show costumes anywhere. 'If I wasn't creating I'd be really unhappy,' she says, as she digs into a pile and comes up with a 'time machine' she has created. 'Steampunk is a Victorian universe in a futuristic world,' she says. 'More is better.' And more there is. More garments to use and more ideas and inspiration for future creations. By some people's standards, Linda might be considered a bit of a hoarder. She even describes herself as being one gene away from the hoarders on TV. 'If I made three a day until I'm ninety, I wouldn't clear all this,' she says, 'but I hate to throw things away.'

When asked about future ideas, she talks excitedly about the spats she will create from leather jackets. She's also collecting duchess sets to make into a quilt, something she has done once before.

Both Linda and Gin belong to a group called LOTSA, an acronym for League of the Splendidly Attired, whose sole purpose is to get together every couple of months, dress up like mad, and go on outings. They have some advice for first-time dressers: 'Always go to the toilet first. If you're wearing a bustle, remember to sit down facing the cistern, and put your boots on before your corset.' The things you have to learn!

Cindy Harvey
Katikati

Master of Dolls

Not having been interested in dolls as a child, I was surprised to find myself absolutely fascinated by a Whitianga doll display. The variety of sizes, styles, expressions, couture and age was staggering. But what fascinated me more than anything else was the incredible attention to detail. Wanting to know more, I went in search of master doll maker, Cindy Harvey.

After raising six children and nursing her mother through terminal illness, Cindy knew: 'It was finally time to do something for me.' Having collected a few mass-produced dolls, Cindy attended doll-making classes in Tauranga and knew she had found her niche. It was an exacting and demanding passion as Cindy chose to make reproduction antique dolls, in which every detail is copied exactly. Initially, Cindy made kitset dolls, but she soon moved into creating the dolls from scratch.

After a number of years Cindy took up an apprenticeship through American doll company Seeley's, which supplies doll-making raw materials. Her training involved numerous three-day workshops with Seeley accredited tutors in various parts of New Zealand. At each workshop she learnt new techniques for painting, firing and clothing the dolls according to the era when they were originally made. It was for one of these workshops that Cindy made Geppetto, Jiminy Cricket

and Pinocchio, complete with extending nose for when he told 'porkies'.

In 2000, Cindy travelled to Melbourne to take her Master's Certificate in Doll Making, where she was given an 1890s doll to recreate. 'This may sound quite easy but right from the beginning it had to be exact,' Cindy explains. 'The underwear, stockings, shoes, corset, and, of course, the outer clothing, hat and shoes, and wig, the crowning glory.'

She gained her Master's, narrowly missing out on a Grand Master's because one eyebrow hair was too long, and because she had used a blended lace rather than a pure cotton, silk or linen lace.

Each doll starts life in the studio where Cindy pours the porcelain slip into a mould. When it is partially dry the excess slip is poured out to create a hollow head, leg, arm or breastplate. Cindy has more than 200 moulds, with dolls measuring anything from a few centimetres high to well over a metre. Once the moulds have dried, they are soft fired in one of the three kilns in Cindy's garage. The face pieces are cleaned and the eye sockets cut out, and then bisque fired for nine hours.

The painting is extremely exacting, built up in layers and fired after each layer. Cindy explains that when the original dolls were made, a left-handed girl would

paint the left eye and a right-handed girl would paint the right eye, meaning that each eye would be quite different. With the goal in antique reproduction to replicate the original doll in every way, it means paying attention to even the smallest detail: the number of eyebrow or eyelash strokes, the length of the strokes, the colour and shape of the blusher, the lip liner and the lipstick.

Once the head has been painted it's ready for the hand-blown glass eyes. Initially using wax to position them, so the eyes can be moved, they are fixed permanently into position with plaster. A pate (the top of the head) is then glued in place, ready for the hair, which is handmade from mohair, Lincoln sheep wool, or human hair. The hair is hand-sewn onto a tape, called wefting, and then hand-sewn onto the head, again matching the thickness of the original doll.

All of this takes place in Cindy's studio, a large room off the back of the garage. The walls are lined with shelves, which as well as housing all her doll-making parts are home to well over 80 dolls. 'The numbers do vary,' she says, 'as some do go to new homes.' There are dolls from all different eras, with different costumes. Amongst them are Cindy's favourites, a striking *Bru 14*, and a lovely *Mein Liebling* (German for my darling). It's like being in a room of beautifully behaved children.

In the centre of Cindy's studio is a large worktable, where Cindy teaches her doll-making classes. A prized possession, her grandmother's treadle sewing machine in full working order, sits beside the doorway, and comes complete with the original sales docket, dated 13 September 1941, for the princely sum of £27. Cindy's first sewing machine, given to her as a child, sits on top.

Once the body of the doll is assembled it's off to Cindy's sewing room, where the high fashion is created. Under the windows is a workbench, which is home to Cindy's overlocker, straight sewer and embroidery machines, while a worktable fills the centre of the room. The shelves are full of beautiful cotton and silk fabrics, arranged in colours, all ready to become the latest couture. 'Fabrics are becoming more difficult to source, especially fine silks and cottons, and cotton laces,' says Cindy, 'I go to second-hand shops in search of christening gowns and wedding dresses, which can be remade into outfits. Sometimes people give me fabric or dresses I can cut down.'

Every doll's outfit is handmade, down to the authentically styled undergarments: camisoles, pantaloons, corsets, and stockings. Stockings are made from old singlets or hand-knitted using one-ply cotton or silk yarns. Shoes are handmade from fine leather. The outfits are all exquisite, with so many added details, trims and fastenings.

I was fascinated by Cindy's explanation of how doll manufacture started. Originally, the dolls were used as mannequins for couture companies. A couturier would dress the doll and send it out to the 'big houses' hoping to tempt the ladies of the house into purchasing gowns from them. When the dolls were not returned to the couturier, enquiries found

that young girls were playing with them. This led to the first dolls being created specifically as playthings in the early 1800s.

Her knowledge is something Cindy is very happy to share. She teaches a couple of nights a week, and has six to eight regular students. The other nights she works on her own dolls. 'I'm not one to watch television,' she says. 'Teaching is really rewarding. I see people come alive. It's a privilege to teach people who want to learn. I know I've found a doll maker when the student starts to talk to their doll, especially when we set the eyes in, as this is when the doll comes to life.

'For a time doll making seemed like a dying art, but as people tire of throwaway thinking and cheap, mass-produced things, these crafts are gaining popularity again and people are realising that what they are crafting will be an 'heirloom' of the future, an object of true beauty. It's so very satisfying, a real confidence builder. In my studio the words "I can't paint" or "I can't do that" are not used, as the desire to do these things will allow you to be taught to do it. It is the greatest therapy there is, and in this pressure-filled world a wonderful stress reliever. My darling husband, Robert, did a lot of pouring of the greenware for the classes and was a huge help and support to my doll-making craft. He was also very interested in the dressing of the dolls and we would discuss what fabrics went together. I miss that interaction so much. Robert passed away on 17 October 2015. I miss him so terribly, but he wanted me to carry on dolly making and teaching others in the beautiful studio that he provided for me.'

Georgia Lines
Pahoia, Katikati

Fresh Talent, Big Dreams

At the young age of 20, Georgia already has some impressive highlights in her chosen career as a singer/songwriter. Emerging as an artist in 2014, Georgia entered the solo/duo section of Smokefree Rockquest. Winning the regionals, she then submitted a 30-minute video of original songs. With no expectations, Georgia was surprised to learn she was in the top 30, and then a week later she found out she was in the top seven in the country. She then played live at the national finals, winning the National Smokefree Woman's Musicianship Award and being named the winner of the solo/duo category. 'Winning was amazing,' she says. 'I got to play to a great crowd, meet some pretty influential people in the music industry, and learn more about what it takes to be a successful artist.'

Anika Moa, one of the judges the year Georgia won, commented: 'She was very entertaining, she dressed well, oozed confidence and is a very good songwriter. Her songs nailed it.' This was not Georgia's first time meeting local musicians, having also performed in Christmas in the Park in Tauranga, meeting artists Tiki Taane, Hollie Smith and Dave Dobbyn.

Another highlight for Georgia was being interviewed by *Uno* magazine. Georgia tells of seeing the magazine in a shop for the first time. 'I had gone into a coffee shop and the *Uno* magazines were spread out on the tables. There was my face looking at me in exactly the same outfit as I was wearing. I quickly bought my coffee and, while I was waiting, went and turned all the magazines face down.'

Unlike Georgia's classmates, who were all going to university, Georgia made the decision to continue working towards her music industry goals. 'I felt the expectation of going to university, but it wasn't for me,' she says. 'I'm not ruling it out, because I always want to be learning and growing and it's one way to do so, but for now I want to write songs, travel and perform.'

Georgia's parents have assisted in renovating a 'sheep shed', making it into a creative space for her to write. Set high up on a bank, with a view over the surrounding fields, it is a peaceful retreat. 'I love people, I love the busyness of life, but I love being by myself creating.'

The far end of the music room is home to her keyboards, a laptop, with Ableton recording software, and a sound system. There's a trestle table, which Georgia sits at in a hammock hung from the ceiling. The centre of the room has shelves, a large antique wardrobe, and a bed for Georgia to crash on during long, night-writing sessions. At the other end is a lounging area, complete with a swing, given to her by her younger brother, also a musician. 'I love this space,' she says, 'I can sit here and just be,' and she points to a comfy, old chair that for a long time was all her studio contained.

Georgia started songwriting in Year 9 when a family friend, Josh Turner, who was teaching her guitar, suggested they should 'write a terrible song'. 'It's easy to sit down with the desire to write something great,

GEORGIA LINES 71

something that's a hit, but when you put that pressure on yourself, often you sit there for hours not knowing where to start.' With no pressure of an outcome, Georgia was soon writing seriously. 'I write about what is happening in my life. It allows me to verbalise how I'm feeling. Often I'll write using chords, which capture the emotion of how I'm feeling. If a lyric can't describe the feeling, a sound or chord progression can.'

Talking of her early days of writing she says she would start with an idea and then make the rest of the story up. 'I think I was afraid to write what I was feeling because I was embarrassed people would know what I actually thought or felt. So I would create these stories around an idea or emotion and hope that the song would make sense. I was writing lyrics to fill the space. But I've realised you can't fill space with a lyric that doesn't mean anything. It loses something; it loses its essence. People relate to how you feel, because the way we feel is universal.' When asked about her writing process, she says she has no set way. 'I often start with the music. I have loads of voice clips on my phone.'

Describing her style as old school rhythm and blues, and nineties hip hop, flavoured with a little early 2000s music, she says, 'It's the chords and the feel of those songs that appeal to me.' Georgia talks about writing in every emotion. 'If you're tired or angry or it's the middle of the night, you write about it when you're experiencing that emotion. There's songs that people will never hear and that's okay.'

Georgia has a clear goal: to write music that makes people feel something, to travel, to tour, and to perform live shows that people say, 'I need to go and see her again.' She talks about the visual and the auditory performance, and the importance of providing both in a live performance.'

It is clear that Georgia has big dreams and is very focused and determined to achieve them, but she also has her feet on the ground. 'It's a business,' she says. 'You have to treat it as a business.' Georgia has organised performances: organising the artists, the venue, the bands, the sound, the tickets and the publicity. She also travels every fortnight to Auckland to attend lessons with voice coach Cheryl McCleay. 'She teaches me laryngeal biomechanics, and how the body works when you sing . . . all things which will help me sustain my voice and help me with my career,' says Georgia.

At the time of the interview Georgia was in the process of recording her first single, *Falling*, and its accompanying music video, working with Olive Jeffares, a New York film-maker who recently moved to Mt Maunganui. Currently working on the storyboards, she says she's really enjoying the visual creative process. When asked who, in the music industry, she would most love to meet, she chooses Kimbra. 'I'd love to meet Beyoncé, but I'd probably just fan-girl over her and ask her to sing for me. Meeting Kimbra would allow me to talk about the business of music. I love the sound she's creating and she works so hard. She's a genius at what she does.'

Jan Fraser-McKenzie

Tauranga

Precious Cargo

If you ever have a few spare moments when in Tauranga, The Cargo Shed is well worth a visit. Sitting on the waterfront, the gallery features over 40 local artists, including leather artist Jan Fraser-McKenzie, whose work is truly unique.

When you first think of leather work, you tend to think of useful items like belts and handbags, but nothing could be further away from Jan's work. She makes the most exquisite sculptures from leather including flowers, leaves, masks and wall hangings. The most exquisite of all her sculptures are her faces.

Jan was first introduced to leather face sculptures by a friend who was making them. She asked for lessons but instead the friend sent her home with some leather telling her to go for it. After some experimenting, Jan was under way.

She starts by making a mould of someone's face using plaster of Paris. From this she makes a papier-mâché mould that she works the leather over, stretching it to create the contours of the face. Jan uses chrome-tanned, light, clothing-weight leathers made from deer, sheep, pigs or calves. All the leather is personally chosen by Jan, who looks for perfect sides without blemishes, or a particular shading or speckle on the soft leather, which makes it unique.

The leather for the faces is 1–1.5 mm thick, making it ideal for achieving special effects such as hair. The detail is incredible, and Jan manages to somehow capture the essence and emotions of each sculpture. I was particularly taken with *Compassion — The Two Marys* on display at The Cargo Shed.

As many of Jan's pieces have a biblical connection, a highlight for her was exhibiting at the Holy Trinity Cathedral in Parnell, Auckland. The exhibition, entitled *Seasons of the Soul*, was an analogy of Christ's time and our time, featuring paintings and leather sculptures. The centrepiece was a spectacular sculpture of Jesus on the cross entitled *The Crucified Christ in Transfiguration*. A life-sized torso draped in white leather representing the transition from the mortal state into immortality, the piece is powerful in its portrayal, detail and expression. It clearly has a deep spiritual meaning for Jan. 'It was the ultimate honour having my work in God's house,' says Jan. This was the first of three exhibitions she held in the cathedral.

Jan also makes leather flower sculptures and a variety of wall hangings. At the time when we met she was working on a pair of doves and a pair of drama masks representing comedy and tragedy. These are all made in thicker vegetable-tanned leather, which she uses because of its 'memory', or ability to hold a shape. In her words, 'This leather is exciting because it has the element of unpredictability!'

The birds are scored with a craft knife to create the feathers. When the leather is wet with very hot water the marks open up to provide the feather detail. Her drama masks were in the process of being painted with acrylic paints, which she says are the accepted paint for leather, although it frequently requires several coats to get the desired effect.

Looking at her work, you might expect that Jan has a fabulous studio tucked away at home. In actual fact all her work is done either at the dining room table or at a small portable table in the lounge. This hasn't always been the case. Jan, along with husband Ken McKenzie, who was also an artist, has owned a number of galleries from which they have both created artwork. In pride of place in her lounge is a large leather sculpture of two faces set into a piece of hakea timber, which came from the farm they were living on in Northland. The piece is called *He Iwi Tahi Tātou*, which translates to 'we are all one people', and seems particularly appropriate as Jan is of Clan Fraser and Ngāti Whanaunga heritage. Jan, like her mother and grandmother, was not raised as Māori, although she says she does know her whakapapa, thanks to her son's work in translating it for the family. She says she never felt like tangata whenua in New Zealand, but on a visit to Scotland she felt it deeply. When asked if she would live there, she replies, 'My family is here.'

It is clear that Jan likes challenges. One of her recent projects was to restore an old leather coat-of-arms. 'It was quite a challenge,' says Jan. 'I'd not done a restoration before, and the colours had to be built up in layers to ensure the best result, but it has been most satisfying to bring an art piece back to its former glory.'

Helen Hagan
Ngaruawahia

Quilter of the Glen

Helen learnt to craft when she was young: picking up hand skills such as knitting, crocheting and embroidery, but it was sewing that gave her a job as well as a lifelong passion. After she left school she worked at Bendon Berlei making lingerie. 'It was great training as I learnt to sew fabrics I wouldn't otherwise have sewn,' she says. She also spent time as a repairs and alterations machinist, and became adaptable to any job.

After raising a family, Helen restarted her crafting journey by attending a course in doll making. It was there she met a quilter who encouraged her to take a quilting course and Helen has been quilting ever since.

Speaking of her hobby/business, Helen says, 'It was never a money-making thing. The business just allowed me to finance my passion for patchwork.' Initially, she intended to use only half the garage, allowing her husband, a radio enthusiast, to use the other half. But when she bought her Nolting Longarm 24" Pro machine, measuring 3.5 metres long, it was clear her husband would have to give up his claim on the garage. The Nolting is a freehand machine, with a throat of 24 inches that can take a king-size quilt. It doesn't have a computer, something Helen says she wouldn't want. 'Where's the creativity in that?' she asks. 'I love being in control, creating the patterns as I go.'

Her first quilt was a sampler made for her daughter. Each square had a different design and featured a different technique she had mastered. She has made many family quilts, including one for each of her two children, one for each of her grandchildren, and one for her parents' fortieth wedding anniversary. Her parents' quilt included photographic panels with wedding pictures, children's pictures and favourite quotes. 'With each quilt I became a bit more adventurous,' she says, moving more into design rather than working from an existing pattern. 'When I design I like to have restful spots in my quilts. That's the artist in me. I spread it out all over the floor. It will sometimes stay there for several days. I just play with it, have fun with it.'

Recently Helen decided it was time to move, but house-hunting was always going to be a bit of a challenge — the big question was where would she fit her longarm sewing machine?

Helen converted a large bedroom into a sewing room adding a quilt-sized pinboard and shelves for some of her considerable stash of fabric — the

garage holds the overflow. In the centre of the room is her longarm machine with just enough space to walk around.

Speaking of her design process she says, 'When I go with the flow, those are the quilts which come out stunning.' She also makes what she calls 'no-think' quilts — using kitsets or pre-printed panels — to give her mind a rest.

Helen also has an overlocker, a blind hemmer, a cover stitch, and a standard sewing machine, which sits on the dining room table. It is here that she does her patchwork and piecing together, before transferring it to the longarm machine for quilting the layers together. Behind the table is a bookcase with an impressive range of quilting books, many of which she has purchased when visiting her children in America or Australia. 'I love the fabrics and books, they are so different from what we see here,' she says, 'and much cheaper.'

Helen is a member of the Church of Jesus Christ of Latter-day Saints and is actively involved in service projects within her church community. A highlight for Helen was organising a quilting workshop for a women's camp in 2013 — many of the more than 100 women who attended had never quilted before. Using gifted and scrap fabrics, and with a number of volunteers to assist, the women tried their hand at a variety of techniques. Helen then completed them on her longarm machine and gifted 17 quilts back to the women in her area. This is just one example of Helen's volunteer work. Helen gifts a quilt to each family in her church on the birth of their first child. 'Ninety per cent of what I make, I give away,' she says.

Another of Helen's growing interests is art quilts. She enjoys reinventing simple shapes and patterns. Helen introduced me to 'zentangling', creating pictures from decorative stitching and patterns, and graffiti quilts made by stitching freehand in a way that is almost like drawing. Helen also enjoys fabric stamping and has experimented with crayon work, and printing onto fabric using a bubble-jet printer.

Helen's 'caring work' extends to handmade thought cards. When someone is going through a difficult time Helen gifts them a scrapbook or visual diary with a beautiful quilted cover, and on a regular basis she delivers handmade 'thought cards' with uplifting messages and sayings. When her husband became ill, she created a visual diary for him, each day writing memories of things they had done, of their children and of their love. It was treasured by her husband, and gave her something to focus on as his illness progressed and after he passed away. 'It still needs finishing,' she says.

Talking of the future, Helen says she has so many ideas. Genealogy is another of Helen's interests. She talks of her Scots ancestry and how she would like to create a Celtic-inspired quilt. She recently bought a new set of colouring books, which she says are great for ideas for stitch patterns for quilts, and would like to get into teaching quilting again. 'It's all about pushing yourself and learning something new,' she says.

Karen Anderson

Hamilton

Through the Looking Glass

How is it that you can teach at the same school with someone for eight years and not know the extent of their publishing career? That was the question I was asking myself as I listened to Karen's story unfold. As well as being an inspirational teacher, Karen has over 160 published book titles, covering 20 different languages.

To enter Karen's 'scriptorium' is to enter her sanctuary. It's where she does her daydreaming and writing, and indulges her love of music. It's also where she houses her treasures, and what else would a writer treasure but books — both those she has written and those of many others. Her collections include two sets of encyclopaedias, the oldest being a set of the *Encyclopaedia Britannica* from 1875 that once resided at the Pukeora Sanatorium in Waipukurau. These found their way to Karen via a second-hand bookshop in the Auckland suburb of Devonport. She also has a set of *Chambers's Encyclopaedia* dating from 1877. What caught my eye, however, were the shelves of *National Geographic* magazines spanning from 1918 to 2000, with only a handful of editions missing. As a child I used to pore over the photos in

these magazines and I'm sure that's where my love of photography was born.

On the wall opposite the *National Geographic* collection stands a similarly handsome selection of early 1900s health, medical and etiquette guides for young ladies, the reading of which is hilarious. But by far the biggest collection, and the one which Karen is absolutely passionate about, is her 1600 different versions of *Alice in Wonderland* including a facsimile copy of an edition that was handwritten by Lewis Carroll. Karen also collects *Alice in Wonderland* figurines and in pride of place in the centre of the room is an *Alice in Wonderland* chess set.

Karen's collections are completed by a seventies and eighties vinyl record collection. When asked how she got into collecting books Karen replied, 'My dad was a collector of vintage bikes and cars, and my mother was a reader and the rest, as they say, is history.'

Karen's own works are inspired by her passion for teaching. All you ever need to know about how to get children reading is there, in the resource books for teachers and in the wonderful children's readers, written to inspire young minds. Karen's teaching resource books, published by Learning Media and

Scholastic Books, have been recommended reading for teachers for many years, spanning reading, writing and mathematics. Her beginner readers, published by Wendy Pye, have been a part of many a young child's journey to a love of books, and have been translated into Finnish, Zulu, French, Mandarin, Samoan, Fijian, Swedish, Mexican, Spanish and Portuguese, to name just a few. Not only does Karen write about literacy, she walks the talk every day in her classroom where she teaches Years 7 and 8. It's interesting, though: the 'scriptorium' is the one room in the house she never takes her schoolwork. 'My golden rule is "no schoolwork allowed",' says Karen.

With so many books you might be tempted to think Karen's scriptorium could be a little fusty, and reminiscent of the book stacks in the basement of your local library, but that couldn't be further from the truth. Karen says she bought the house because of this room. It has a warm ambience about it, which invites you in and suggests you pause a while. This is, in part, due to the lovely big ranchsliders framing the view outside, as well as the furniture, which has been chosen with care. There is a particularly nice restored rimu cabinet,

which spent its youth as the ticket cabinet for the Hunterville railway station. The ultimate writer's workstation in the form of a retro-style desk houses more quirky treasures, including a brass compass and microscope, and a phrenology bust. The bust is a miniaturised head used for the nineteenth-century pseudo-science of phrenology, which focused on the measurements of the human skull as a diagnostic tool.

When I asked Karen how she got started in writing, she explained that she was given 19 out of 20 by her Form 2 teacher for a story she had written, and she has never looked back. It just goes to show how influential teachers can be!

Karen also has a garden shed and woodworking garage that would rival any bloke's shed, with a range of tools including a drop saw, saw bench, drill press, planers and routers. This is where Karen challenges herself to build things for the garden, including a fully enclosed raised garden bed, planter boxes, a weather station and a cat play station, which perversely her cats refuse to play on unless she's working on it. Again her thirst for knowledge takes over. 'What do I need to learn to solve it?' she says, then thinks for a moment. 'Oh golly, I might have to make a trip to Mitre 10!'

Clare Wimmer

Waitetuna, Waikato

Lighting the World

Clare is a woman of many ideas. She works as the business manager for CLIMsystems, a company which consults on climate adaptation and risk. She raises her own food, both animal and vegetable, and lives in an eco-friendly mud-wall house designed and built by her husband, David.

Along with their two boys, five sheep, two kunekune pigs, eight rabbits bred for eating, and five chickens, Clare lives on a one-hectare farmlet at Waitetuna, west of Hamilton. There is a common thread to everything she does, and she talks enthusiastically about her passions: 'earth care', 'people care' and 'fair share', the basic tenants of permaculture and sustainability. She is also a ceramic artist, which is how I came to meet her.

Set amongst the potager vegetable garden is Clare's pottery studio, somewhere, she says, she doesn't get to spend enough time. The studio is a generous size, attached to a large barn. It is where the family first lived when they moved to the property 11 years ago. Now it's Clare's space. As she says, 'I don't have a space in the house — everyone else does but I don't. This is where I can come that's mine. I know where everything is.'

The front room, which is a real suntrap, is set up with a weathered dining table and chairs that beckons comfort and a morning cup of coffee. It's a

great place to dry clothes, but an even lovelier place to look out on the garden and gain creative inspiration. Behind this lies the clay studio, where the messy stuff happens. 'Working with clay is meditation for me,' says Clare.

Clare was first introduced to ceramic art in Nashua, New Hampshire, where she volunteered at an art gallery. After finishing work she would head downstairs to play in the clay studio. A few years later, working for Pots A Plenty in Sydney, Clare extended her pottery skills and, in particular, learnt how to make money from creating clay work.

Clare has a postgraduate diploma in business research, a diploma in ceramic art, and a permaculture design certificate through Permaculture in New Zealand (PiNZ). Most recently, she has been studying sustainable marketing. Teaching also fits with Clare's ethos. Sitting on the bench are a number of small pots — works in progress of a group of overseas students she is mentoring under the masters internship programme at the University of Waikato. They've come to try their hand at pottery, something they say they would never get a chance to do in their home countries. Clare was also instrumental in setting up the Raglan Clay Shed Community Pottery and she has worked with Creative New Zealand on their grants committee.

But Clare's real passion is working in porcelain, a fine white clay known for its strength. From this she creates delicate, lacy light fixtures, which cast the most beautiful wall patterns when switched on. The lights are firstly extruded using a porcelain paper clay made in her studio. Some sections are slip cast and others are turned on the wheel then

assembled before firing and glazing. Clare also creates figurines from porcelain, her latest being a range of angels. I am particularly intrigued by a set of handmade wood-fired worm pots, which slot nicely one on top of the other, turning vegetable scraps into compost by worm action.

The last two rooms of Clare's space hold the kiln and a showroom. There are only a few pieces on the shelves as most of her work is in galleries. Increasing her production is something Clare would like to change when time permits — especially focusing on products that encourage sustainability. She has plans to create orb-like vessels for watering the garden, encouraging the sustainable use of our most precious resource. Buried under the ground, these semi-porous pots gradually leach water into the soil. She is also interested in creating vessels for the natural fermentation of food and drinks like sauerkraut and kombucha.

Clare is blessed with bucket-loads of 'start up' energy, and like most energisers finds balancing multiple priorities and having time to do the things she loves a bit of a challenge. I get the impression that if I come back in five years' time, I would see enormous progress. Whether it is in the garden or the pottery, I am sure sustainability will be Clare's central theme.

Susan Flight
Raglan

Mountain Dreaming

When Susan Flight returned from Australia as a widow, she was looking for a place to put down roots. Having always been drawn to New Zealand's west coast beaches, Susan travelled the North Island looking for a new place to call home, a place to indulge her artistic passion for ceramics, and a place that would just feel right. It was during this travel time that Susan came to the conclusion that she didn't want a house, she really wanted a shed — a place she could put her own creative stamp on. She found it 15 minutes from Raglan, nestled on the slopes of Mt Karioi. It was a run-down shearing shed in need of loads of TLC, but with a view to die for across rolling farmland to distant views of Aotea Harbour. After negotiating a long-term lease with the farmer, Susan set about renovating it, well, actually gutting it and turning it into the creative home and ceramics studio she calls Mountain Dreaming Arts Workshop.

The top floor is huge and completely open, apart from the bathroom. Everything happens in this space. It acts as kitchen, dining, lounge, bedroom and office. At every turn there is something to catch your eye: a piece of Susan's artwork or something she's collected on her travels. Susan has a flair for display. Amongst the usual household items of couches and bookshelves,

Susan has placed multiple white plinths to display her handcrafted ceramics. There's an amazing variety of pieces, including figurines and animals, each piece with a story to tell and a place in the timeline of Susan's crafting.

Susan has set aside a large area downstairs for her workroom and teaching studio. It's a great space with individual workstations and room for people to walk around. Down a few steps to the right is the glazing and firing room, with a pyrometric-controlled kiln that she can set and walk away, and a small glass kiln that sits alongside her partner's home brew kit. Outside, there is a raku kiln, in which pieces are fast fired to 1000°C, then removed from the kiln hot and put into sawdust to create a chemical reaction. Both downstairs areas have the feel of grown-ups' messy play areas, which is very much in line with Susan's teaching style.

Susan has a long history in artistic endeavour. Leaving her safe job at Thames High School, at the age of 40, Susan went into artwork full-time. She created textiles, wall panels and fashion, including hand-dyed silk, which was sought after for evening gowns and featured in the Benson & Hedges Fashion Design Awards. Soon she was after a new challenge though. When Susan moved to Australia she completed a ceramics course at the Sunshine Institute, and later set up a teaching studio in Neerdie, on the Sunshine Coast, which she ran for 12 years.

Susan's CV is testament to her work ethic. 'I just see myself as a worker. What I love, I work at. The end result is out of my control.' The end result has,

however, been highly successful. Susan has won numerous New Zealand and Australian awards and study grants, and through the 1990s she was in demand as an adjudicator for textile and fibre competitions. Susan has also illustrated a number of books and worked as an arts reviewer, writing for both newspapers and magazines. Most impressive of all, however, is the list of exhibitions she's been involved in, both in Australia and New Zealand, which spans the 1970s until today. She marked her return to New Zealand with an exhibition, *Where the Magpie Sings*, at Hamilton's Arts Post in 2009.

On the day I met Susan she was running her regular one-day-a-month class. The group had just finished an exhibition at the Raglan Arts Centre, and were happy to share their thoughts. 'Susan gets us started on something, then let's us put our own stamp on it,' says one. 'Susan is so giving of her time and expertise,' says another. 'She critiques our work honestly and kindly.' 'She has a great sense of humour.' The praise is high and genuinely felt. Everyone's got their own reason for attending. 'It's an escape for me.' 'It's been like a private club, but I got in.' There is clearly more than just clay work being done here.

A year ago Susan made the decision to wind things down a little, the once-a-month group and a summer school being the only teaching Susan now does. 'At my age I choose what I want to do.'

Reflecting on her time as an artist Susan says, 'It's a tremendous state of privilege, doing what you want to do, and if you have enough money to get by, that's bloody nice too.'

Staying Passionate about Being Creative

All the ladies I have interviewed will tell you they had times when their creative energy waned and they had to find ways to revitalise their creativity. Below are a number of strategies that may work for you.

Clear Away 'Buts'

If there is something blocking your way, figure out what it is. Ask yourself if it is 'real'. If it is, find a solution. Don't ignore it. If it is real, it's not going to go away.

Check out your inner dialogue. If the negative voice in your head is telling you that you couldn't, shouldn't, or wouldn't be able to do whatever you are attempting, ask yourself where these thoughts come

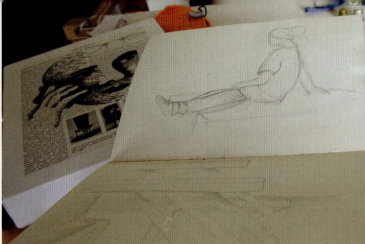

from. The best way to deal with past put-downs or a lack of confidence is to go out and do it anyway. You wouldn't expect your child to get good at playing an instrument without practising, so give yourself the same opportunity. Practise something until you get good at it.

If you have a knowledge gap blocking you, head to the library, go online, ask a retailer, talk to someone in your local arts and crafts group, or just experiment and find out for yourself. Keep asking the question; eventually you will find the answer.

If time is the issue, make a date with yourself every week. We have all the time we can get, it's our choices as to how we use it that need to change. If family and friends are struggling with your taking time out, talk to them about why it's important to you, and how they can support you. If they're still not happy, do it anyway. You will be setting a great example for your children in following your passion.

If money is the issue, think about how you could recoup some of your expenses. Can you sell some? Could you teach someone? Can you make a gift rather than buying one? Can you swap with someone to get what you need? Check out some of the marketing strategies in the section called 'The M Words — Marketing and Money' (page 187).

If you are having trouble getting started, think about where you left off last time. I have found it beneficial to always leave my work with an easy thing to do as the next step, rather than something I'm unsure of or I find difficult. That way the work is easy to pick up and get started on, and once you start you can then tackle the difficult bit.

Turn Up

There's no way out of this one. You have to show up and put the time in, even if it is just pottering around in the space. Eventually this will lead to positive action.

Commit yourself to one positive action each day — putting in a few stitches, making a phone call, tidying your space. If you do nothing, nothing will change.

Create a ritual around starting work in your space each day. It could include a cup of coffee, sitting in your favourite chair creating a plan, talking to the cat or dog. It doesn't matter what it is, but when you do it every day it signals to your brain that it's time to start work.

Deal with procrastination by making deadlines and sticking to them. If this is a challenge, make it harder on yourself to bow out by sharing those deadlines with someone else.

Be organised. Nothing gets in the way of creativity more than a 'to do' list that's bugging you to do something, and doing something creative is a great way to reward yourself for being on top of your game.

Keep your space tidy-ish. I say tidy-ish because I like to have stuff out around me when I create, but there's a fine line between that and a chaotic jumble, which does my head in.

Build Your Creative Energy

Teach someone something, no matter how small. When they ask you something you don't know, research it. You never know, it could open up a whole new field of opportunity for you.

Try a 100-day challenge. Create something every day for 100 days. They say it takes 30 days to create a new habit. Do it for 100 just to be safe.

Open your mind to inspiration in your everyday life. Collect bits and pieces and ideas, then ask yourself, 'What could I do with this?' When writing songs I used to open the dictionary randomly and search for a starter word. Where could you get starter ideas from? Stay open to new influences. Most people's creative style evolves over time.

Look to the past. Your memories, family traditions, and rituals hold a wealth of ideas.

Take a trip to your local supply shop. You're bound to be tempted with something that can keep your creative juices flowing.

Touching your dream builds motivation. Whatever you dream about doing creatively, imagine it, then go and find it. If it's a new gizmo to make something, research it or go and look at it. Ask yourself, 'What would I have to do to be able to get this?'

Surround yourself with other creatives. Have creative play dates in someone else's space. Exchange ideas. They don't have to be interested in the same thing as you. Creative spin-off could come from someone working in an entirely different field.

Join an online chat group, follow a blog or Pinterest account, or follow a Twitter account or subject hashtag, for example, #artist, #creative. Regular email alerts will remind you that there are others out there doing it, so why not you? They could also be a great source of ideas.

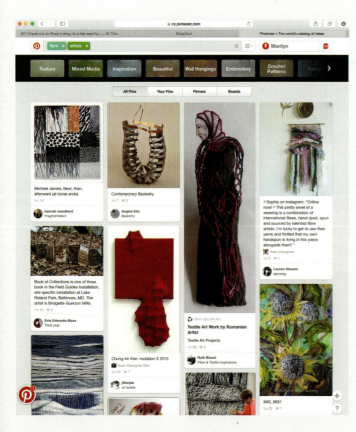

Take a sketchbook or notepad wherever you go. You never know when inspiration will strike, and while we think we will remember those great ideas, the reality is we often don't.

Be open to collaboration.

Purposely set aside playtime for experimenting without the expectation of making useable work. Try something new. Ask what if I combined, shrank, upsized, or did this with a new medium? Use a set of creativity cards, and randomly turn a card over and do whatever it tells you to do.

Above all, don't overthink it. Get your head out of the game and just let it flow.

Jill Matthew
Cambridge

Life's Too Short

At the age of 29, newly married and with everything to look forward to, Jill Matthew was struck down by a crippling neurological condition, transverse myelitis with encephalitis. Overnight she went from feeling a little off to not being able to walk, talk or see. An extensive physical therapy and rehabilitation programme followed. Her recovery took nearly two years and she found her life had taken a drastic U-turn.

During the early part of her illness, Jill made the decision to resign from her job as a practice nurse manager. She had no idea what she wanted to do — she just knew that 'life is too short.' In her search for something to relieve the boredom, Jill recalled a one-hour flame-working course she had done a few years before. 'I loved melting and manipulating the glass. It planted a seed, although at the time, I didn't expect to follow through'.

Looking for something to focus on during her recovery period, she ordered a glass-melting torch and a microwave oven-sized kiln, and started creating. 'I might be able to do something with this,' she thought. Initially, Jill created jewellery. For her thirtieth birthday, her husband presented her with a bigger kiln, which enabled Jill to work with larger pieces. She started experimenting with fused glass platters, cutting and layering glass, and fusing it in a kiln.

Using the goal-setting skills that had been so valuable during her rehabilitation, Jill set herself the goal of having her work in a gallery somewhere by the end of the year. She accomplished this three months early. 'It was a huge learning curve, with very little support in the way of courses in New Zealand.'

Crediting Google as her go to place for information, Jill researched the science and the art of fused glass. 'It's quite scientific and quite process based,' she says. 'I had to learn about coefficients of expansion, how to avoid building up stress within the glass, and where to source glass that would expand at the same rate.'

All Jill's pieces, including the shaped ones, start life as flat pieces of glass, which she then layers up. 'I'm a systematic person,' she says. 'I'm much more of a constructor than a "traditional" artist. I never write down a plan for a piece. I just go and build one. Sometimes it takes five minutes, sometimes it takes a few days.'

Once layered, the piece is fired — usually for 24 hours as it has to be slowly warmed up and cooled down to prevent 'shocking' the glass. Once cooled, it is then re-fired in a mould to give it its final shape. Each of her eye-catching pieces is unique. 'I love that I couldn't reproduce it even if I tried.'

While she has some more easily produced items, like her personalised Christmas decorations, Jill has made a conscious decision to position herself in the art-glass market. She says she is inspired by nature, and the special qualities of glass, and she is never short of ideas.

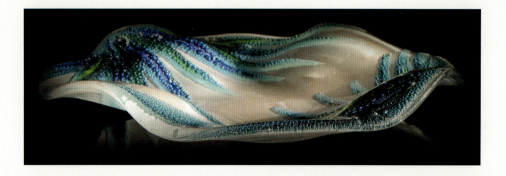

Jill also works with metal powders, which she sandwiches between layers of glass. These create the most gorgeous swirling patterns. 'Glass is very particular when using metal powders. You never know what you are going to get. You can foresee it but you can never accurately predict it,' she says.

Jill has two workspaces, which was a huge deciding factor when she and her husband purchased their house in Cambridge. 'Downstairs is where the magic happens: the planning, the cutting, and the piecing together. It's where I get inspired.'

Opposite her large worktable is a pigeonhole shelf where Jill stores the huge variety of glass she works with. It's a functional and well-organised space, with her finished glassware and her School Certificate art boards being the only giveaways that this is an artistic space.

A set of stairs leads to her second space — the kiln room. Jill currently has three kilns, one for each of the firings, and a recently acquired, bigger kiln, which allows her to complete much larger pieces of glass art. The room also houses Jill's substantial collection of moulds used to shape her final products. On the wall are two pieces entitled *Summer Hugs* and *Winter Kisses*, which are good examples of Jill's dynamic use of colour and texture.

Jill's business background has helped her shape her business. She started at the height of the recession and, as people's disposable income grew, Jill's business grew. She sells her work through Facebook and through galleries in about equal proportion. She monitors what she sells and where, and is conscious of having a balance of more commercial lines and her exclusive art pieces.

Monika Neuhauser

Pirongia

A Day at the Races

On entering Monika's studio I was immediately transported back to my rag-trade days, reliving the excitement of fashion being created. So many things caught my eye, from glamorous finished hats in all shapes, shades and sizes, to fabrics, feathers, beads, ribbons, bows and flowers. Her showroom is filled with ready-to-wear hats. Every hat is different, and I found myself wishing I had been brave enough to wear hats when I was young. To the left of the showroom is Monika's workroom, with hats at varying stages of completion, and an array of tools and machines.

Monika and her husband first came to New Zealand on their honeymoon and returned to settle shortly after their first daughter was born. Her hat-making journey started when a friend invited her to the races. Assured by her friend that it was a glamorous occasion that called for an equally glamorous hat, Monika went shopping, but to no avail, arriving home empty handed. Being both practical and determined, and with the aid of Google, Monika sat down and made her first hat. From that first hat her business began, as one after another of her friends asked her to make hats for them. These days Monika has an excellent reputation amongst the racing fraternity, and I was

encouraged to visit her earlier rather than later in the year as the racing season, which runs from late August until April, keeps her very busy. Fashion is big business at the races, Monica explains. 'Prizes can range from a goody bag at small races, to driving away in a brand new AU$75,000 Lexus, part of an overall prize pool of more than AU$400,000 at the Melbourne Fashion in the Fields last year.'

For a long time, Monika was self-taught, then in 2012 she attended an Australian International Millinery Convention and in her words, 'It was a life changer. Being immersed in all sorts of materials, attending workshops and meeting others as passionate about hat making as me was inspirational. My creativity expanded in ways I couldn't previously have imagined.'

Not long after the conference, Monica moved her hat-making business into the guestroom, attached to the garage. She started in a corner and gradually expanded. 'I've been like a fungus, creeping in and taking over. Now the whole space is mine. It's my sanctuary. I own every corner and enjoy every minute in here. I think I'm so lucky to have this.' And it's easy to see why. Favourite possessions are displayed here as well as the trappings of her trade, which Monika surrounds herself with when she's creating.

Being a Virgo, Monika says she should be orderly, but that's not her. She likes to pull things out, and doesn't stop to tidy up until the mess gets to the point where it inhibits her creative process. On the wall in the showroom is a print from an 1834 fashion magazine, given to her by a friend. Another favourite of Monika's, is a ceramic figurine of the Venus of Willendorf, an ancient figure that dates back to about 28000 BC, which was discovered in Austria in 1908. Appropriately, the figurine is one of the earliest known symbolic figures to have a hat.

The tools of Monika's trade are also on show, including a 1952 Singer sewing machine, her vintage French flower-making tools, and an array of hat blocks. Included in her collection are two blocks that date back to the 1920s, while many of the other blocks have been hand-turned by Monika's husband.

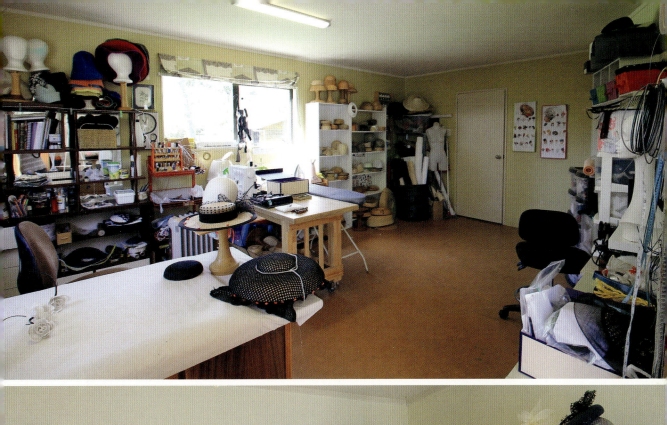

Monika's collection of hat boxes and vintage fabrics has been much added to by finds on online auction sites, including some incredibly soft rabbit's felt, which she says 'moulds like butter'. Another favourite fabric, called esparterie, was traditionally made from willow fibre then covered in gauze. According to Monika, the traditional version has a richness and quality to it that is missing in the modern version of gauze-covered paper.

I was really curious about how Monika worked with clients, particularly when making bespoke hats. Did she ever have clients, like me, who had never worn a hat and didn't want to 'stick out in the crowd'?

'These are typically the mother of the bride,' she says. Her standard reply is, 'You're the mother of the bride, of course you're going to be obvious!' She then sets about getting them to try hats on, coaching and coaxing until the lady sees that indeed she can wear a hat and feel great doing so.

Last year Monika decided she wanted to open a shop in Hamilton, so that she could be seen and have people drop in. When the reality of running a shop set in — overheads, interruptions, no flexibility of hours — she backed away. Now she is happy enjoying her Pirongia paradise. 'I love seeing my garden, the dogs, the cats and the birdlife. I love every season and every day is enjoyable.'

Gerlinde Weinzettl

Pirongia

Skid Row

The first thing you see when you come down the driveway to Gerlinde's house is her studio. Nestled amongst large deciduous trees, it is the cutest 'she shed' ever with its high-pitched roof and spacious veranda. It hasn't always been here though. A neighbour just down the road was selling it, and Gerlinde's husband was very keen to move her out of 'his' garage so he bought it. Being an engineer, he decided that they could move the whole thing down the road on skids. And so they did. The local village fire brigade was called in to stop the traffic, and to spray water on the road so the studio would slide more easily as it was towed by tractor to its new location. The whole neighbourhood turned out to watch, except Gerlinde. She was looking after the children, but really that was just an excuse not to be there as she was too afraid to watch in case something happened. Nothing did, of course, and Gerlinde then set about making it her artistic home.

    The studio is a warm and inviting space, with golden, natural timber and a hint of fairytale with a ladder to the loft. Gerlinde says of her space, 'I feel enclosed. It gives me a hug. I can lock the door. I can make a mess and it doesn't matter'.

Gerlinde studied ceramics at school in Austria. It was a comprehensive course, including tiling and building 'mansion stoves' (called kachelofen) with specialised ceramic linings. Initially, when she came to New Zealand ceramics was a hobby, which she did tucked away in the corner of the family garage. Then Gerlinde enrolled in a Te Wānanga o Aotearoa visual arts course, entitled Toi Rauangi. 'I wanted something local,' she says. 'I was trying to understand. They were so welcoming.'

Gerlinde then went on to Wintech to finish a media arts degree in sculpture and painting. 'The most important thing I learned there was to look for the story behind the artwork.'

Each of her pieces has a story, like the *Flying Pig*, whose inspiration lay in a mother pig that would throw her piglets out of the way to get to the food. It happened so often the flying piglets became a family joke, and the sculpture was created to capture the shared story. Another animal piece is based on Gerlinde's horse, a Haflinger, which is an Austrian breed renowned for their large posteriors.

Many of Gerlinde's pieces have a Māori influence, like her patupaiarehe, the fairies of Mt Pirongia, each of which she has gifted its own name. Most impressive of all is the commissioned work of a Māori kaitiaki, or guardian, a companion for a previous sculpture of *Kahupekarere*, who gave Mt Pirongia its name. At the time I visited, the kaitiaki sculpture was drying, before being

kiln fired. It is both imposing and inspiring at the same time. As with many of Gerlinde's pieces, I found that I wanted to touch it and connect with its story.

Gerlinde is also working on a series of tusks, which she is decorating with traditional Austrian and Māori motifs, some of which she says are quite similar. The tusks are a move away from the softer, more feminine forms that Gerlinde has created in the past.

Asked how a European woman comes to be making Māori art she says, 'I never say I do Māori art, because I am not Māori. But I am inspired by Māori art.'

Many of her pieces are made in white raku clay from Australia. She particularly likes this clay for its strength and ability to seamlessly join parts to make large works. This is important as Gerlinde builds everything as she goes rather than hollowing out pieces after she makes them.

She experiments with a variety of glazes and techniques including oxide washes, compressor-sprayed glazes and raku glazing, where the object is taken out of the kiln red hot and placed into sawdust, which draws out the colour. Her next move will be to try printing on clay using a silk screen, something she saw on a recent trip overseas.

When we met, Gerlinde was studying business management. She realises that side of things is necessary, but says she would really rather just be creating. In the future she hopes to do more installations and exhibitions but who knows? As she says, 'Sometimes I see what I want to do, other times it just flows out of my hands.'

Nynke Piebenga
Pirongia

A River at My Door

Nynke and her husband live on a beautiful, rolling 28-hectare countryside property. Nynke's weaving studio is a purpose-built room within their home. The view from one weaving loom sweeps across the garden to the Waipa River, and from the other loom you can see across the fields to Mt Pirongia. The views alone would give anyone creative inspiration. Nynke calls this property small, and it is in comparison to their previous property — a sheep farm of 690 hectares at Mahoenui, near Te Kuiti. It was at the farm that Nynke's weaving story started.

Living in an isolated rural community with little to do, Nynke decided to take weaving lessons. When she saw a smoke-damaged loom for sale cheap, Nynke jumped at the chance to buy it. She has never looked back.

In the early days, she put her first loom in an empty house on the property, and in the afternoons when the children were napping she'd retreat to her space and work on her weaving. Occasionally, she would go to the local spinners and weavers group, but she never got into spinning, always preferring to weave.

Like most of the house, Nynke's studio has a warm ambience with plenty of natural light. The rimu rafters and mouldings were taken from a tree felled on their Mahoenui property. She now has two large looms in her studio, as well as another two tabletop looms that she uses to make smaller pieces or when she is travelling to demonstrations and exhibitions. The room is a perfect setting for the looms, which in themselves are works of art, made in rimu with turned wood and brass fittings. There is an alcove for a work desk and Nynke's extensive book collection, and large areas of wall space for displaying Nynke's treasured pieces. Tucked behind a wall is a staircase leading to a loft area where Nynke stores her yarns. Everything has been thought of with the same attention to detail that Nynke crafts into her woven pieces.

Knowing little about weaving I needed a quick lesson and Nynke patiently explained the workings of the two big looms. The larger of the two is an eight-shaft countermarche loom. The action of this loom is quite complicated. When you push the treadle down, some of the warp ends go up and some go down. In comparison, on Nynke's smaller jack loom, the chosen warp ends only lift up. The countermarche loom is great for getting even tension, which is particularly useful when a firm tension is required. It is, however, more complicated to tie up when getting started. Nynke enjoys being able to move from one loom to the other, as she sits differently at each one allowing her to ease her muscles.

Nynke uses a wide range of materials including wool, linen,

silk and cotton, but she doesn't restrict herself to traditional yarns. One of her latest pieces is woven using the inner tubes of bicycle tyres. If you look closely at the photo you can even see the manufacturer's stamps on the bag and cushion. This work has earned her a commission for a long bench seat for a Melbourne restaurant. In 2015, Nynke won the Perendale Sheep Breeders of New Zealand Breeders' Award at the Creative Fibre New Zealand awards. The prize included a Perendale fleece, which she has made into the softest, most luxurious rug in two shades of blue, hand-dyed in her kitchen.

For me the biggest surprise of all were Nynke's curtains, made from metres of handcrafted fabric — wool in the weaving room, cotton and Tencel in the lounge, and linen upstairs. Nynke has woven the fabric and then sewed the curtains! They are simply a work of art hanging on the walls to be drawn at the end of each day, beautifully complementing the natural timber finish in their home.

There are many treasured pieces on the walls in Nynke's studio, each one telling a story of its own. Above her large loom is a piece collected while in Ethiopia. Nynke and a friend spent six weeks there teaching young women in impoverished living conditions to weave. For these girls the experience would have been life-changing as they had been given a way to make a living. The two flax woven pieces are particularly significant to Nynke — a kete made by Dame Rangimārie Hetet and a pōtae, or sunhat, made by her daughter Diggeress Te Kanawa. Nynke attended a flax-weaving course with Diggeress, where they harvested the flax, prepared it for weaving, then created a finished product. On the wall by the stairs hangs another Māori weaving piece, a sampler made by Dame Rangimārie's granddaughter, Kahutoi Te Kanawa (see page 113), which was commissioned by a friend as a gift for Nynke.

Nynke has established quite a reputation for herself in the world of weaving, and has put back many hours into the Creative Fibre organisation holding various official positions including Education Officer, National President, and Exhibition Officer. She is also in demand as a weaving tutor. Nynke sells her work and gains commissions through word of mouth. 'I am just as passionate about my weaving now as I was forty years ago. There is still so much to learn and explore,' says Nynke.

Kahutoi Te Kanawa
(Ngāti Maniapoto)
Te Kuiti

Māwhitiwhiti — a Weaving Legacy

While I was interviewing Nynke Piebenga (see page 109), she showed me three pieces of traditional Māori weaving by three members of the same family: grandmother, Dame Rangimārie Hetet; mother, Diggeress Te Kanawa; and daughter, Kahutoi Te Kanawa. I was fascinated by their story and decided I needed to know more, which is how I met Kahutoi. Hers is a story of a weaving legacy.

Until recently, Kahutoi Te Kanawa was the co-ordinator of the Masters of Applied Indigenous Knowledge course at Te Wānanga o Aotearoa. Coming from a family renowned for their weaving knowledge, Kahutoi says, 'I was very fortunate to be brought up with passionate people around me. My mother, Diggeress, who had been named after the diggers in World War One, was creative in many areas: sewing, cake making, gardening and weaving.'

At the time of the interview Kahutoi was working on a traditional cloak, sitting in her lounge at a large leather armchair, her weaving mounted on a wooden frame with the long fibres tucked into a cotton sheet. As Kahutoi explained and demonstrated the weaving to me, it was clear the work held a deep spiritual meaning. In no time her handwork had taken on a steady and relaxing rhythm. It is patient and time-consuming work.

From where Kahutoi sits weaving, she can look up to the photo gallery on the wall — photos of her grandmother, mother and extended family. She remembers the strong role models of Rangimārie and Diggeress. 'They were hardworking, humble, gentle, kind, wise and very knowledgeable. How can you not be creative when you are surrounded by it, by innovation, creativity and logic?'

As a child Kahutoi says she was never allowed to waste time. 'No idle hands,' she says. 'We were always busy and we all had chores.' This is hardly surprising as Kahutoi is one of 12 children. She remembers holidays with Nana: 'You'd be preserving, crocheting, doing needlepoint, weaving or gardening. We learnt how to be innovative, and we learnt to try and try again. Most important of all, we learnt how to have truthful relationships. We trusted and cared for each other.'

Learning to weave was never something that was forced on Kahutoi. Initially, she learnt by osmosis, picking up skills and techniques just by being around Diggeress and Rangimārie. Gradually, over a period of 15–20 years, Kahutoi moved from observer to helper, to working on her own. 'Whatever our parents were doing we observed and followed,' she says. Working alongside them, Kahutoi learnt the language of raranga (flax weaving) and grew to

understand the patterns, colours, techniques and precision of raranga and whatu (fibre weaving).

During the fifties, kākahu (cloak) weaving had been in serious decline. Through the Māori Women's Welfare League, Rangimārie and Diggeress passed on their knowledge of weaving, which was a departure from the customary practice of teaching only within their own tribe.

Rangimārie's weaving was distinguished by a crossover pattern called māwhitiwhiti, the pattern becoming part of the Hetet family's weaving legacy. Just as her grandmother and mother before her, Kahutoi has worked hard to preserve the knowledge and skills of Māori weaving, particularly in her various roles at Te Wānanga o Aotearoa.

Kahutoi is glad these skills are being passed on, but a little saddened that it is within the confines of tertiary institutions. 'My great-grandmother experienced the land wars, my grandmother two world wars, my mother had to relearn her own language,' she says. 'These are some of the stories we shared while we were weaving.'

Kahutoi is currently studying for her doctorate, undertaking research exploring the intergenerational transfer of mātauranga raranga whatu (knowledge of flax weaving and fibre weaving). As part of her study Kahutoi will be working to recreate a piece of weaving held in the Otago Museum, made by an unknown weaver. In this way she hopes to understand the story about the piece and how it came to be, most importantly showing how the innate knowledge of weaving can continue through the practice of raranga.

Like Rangimārie and Diggeress, Kahutoi has exhibited, presented and run workshops, demonstrating at national and international museums and universities. She has served as an executive committee member, including a term as vice president of the Te Roopu Raranga Whatu o Aotearoa Komiti (National Māori Weavers Committee), an organisation co-founded by Diggeress in the early eighties.

Highlights for Kahutoi have been numerous, including being able to work and exhibit alongside her grandmother and mother at Waitomo in the late 1980s at a family run business. From June 2014 to July 2015 the Waikato Museum hosted a five-generation exhibition including work by Kahutoi's great-grandmother, Mere Te Ronga Pamamao, her grandmother Dame Rangimārie, her mother, Diggeress, her sisters, Ria Davis and Rangituatahi Te Kanawa, her niece, Clowdy Ngatai, and Veranoa Hetet, daughter of her first cousin. Kahutoi's work was also part of the exhibition. The museum is entrusted with the Hetet/Te Kanawa collection. Diggeress made cloaks for 11 of her children and a wall hanging for one of her sons who had already been given his cloak by Dame Rangimārie. Kahutoi also collaborated with Dr Ngahuia Te Awekotuku, Waikato Museum staff and other family members to produce a book, entitled *E Ngā Uri Whakatupu — Weaving Legacies*, to accompany the exhibition.

Judi Brennan

Taupo

A Magic Garden

Judi grew up in a creative household. 'My mother was into all sorts of art and we always had everything we needed to be artistic.' Originally wanting to be a fashion designer, Judi found her passion for ceramics by accident in the early seventies. After being in the waiting list for a long time, Judi's sister was finally given a place in a pottery night class. By then she'd moved to Australia so Judi took her place instead and in her words, 'I couldn't get enough of it.'

Judi's first studio was in the stable on a farm in Colyton near Feilding. She worked mainly with oxides making clay boots, big pottery houses with lights, and lighthouses, which she sold through local markets and a few shops. Attending a Feilding night class, she mastered the potter's wheel, but was always drawn to hand building of ceramics. 'I love to push the boundaries,' she says. 'I'm always thinking what if I add this . . . what if I tried that?'

Judi continued her ceramic work when she moved to Acacia Bay extending her range to include kiwis, owls and Big Bird, plant pets and Hucklebugs. Another move saw the introduction of her hugely successful range of tableware, square nested plates and sloped cups. It was around this time that Judi found a book by the Austrian artist and architect Friedensreich

Hundertwasser — best known in this country for the public toilets he created in Kawakawa — and became inspired to create mosaics.

In 1997 she moved to her current location, a one-hectare section in Mapara Road, where she started the Clay Art Studio selling directly to the public. For a time she continued making the dinnerware but changed to mosaics soon after. 'I had built a path up to the studio, embedding little clay cats, fish and dogs into it. There was so much interest in these little pieces, we started making them, turning the Clay Art Studio into a mosaic place where we held workshops and sold supplies.'

In 2005, having sold the Clay Art Studio, Judi and her daughter, Jo, set up their café, L'Arté, later adding a creative studio and gallery to it. 'When the café first opened I was creating at night, running the shop from the café, and helping out in the kitchen. It was hectic and I felt a little lost without a dedicated space to work in. Looking back I don't know what I was thinking,' she laughs. 'After a couple of years I moved into the garage and added the gallery space.'

Judi has unleashed her creativity to create a spectacular, larger than life mosaic living room in the garden. If you ever wondered how Alice in Wonderland felt after drinking the 'shrink me' potion, take a seat in the contoured couch or try out the magnificent armchair. It's a delightful 'return to childhood' experience.

Strolling around the magical gardens, I come across many of Judi's brightly coloured ceramics: bird houses, sculptural towers, bird baths and ceramic flowers. A short walk up the garden path, over the mosaic stepping-stones, is Judi's gallery and behind it the workroom. It is here that the magic happens. Judi's space is full of inspiration and temptations to purchase, including her quirky teapots with their signature style.

The workroom is a T-shaped space with an adjoining kitchenette. There is a large central worktable where the hand building is done. To the left are floor-to-ceiling racks for raw materials and work-in-progress storage, and to the right are shelves of finished product. It is a well organised and orderly space, set up for efficient production. The electric kiln is located in a separate shed out the back.

L'Arté is closed on Mondays and Tuesdays (except in January and on public holidays), which allows Judi the time and freedom to do her own thing. 'I'm never short of ideas,' she says, 'just short of time. I work in little windows

of creativity. It's great to be successful commercially, but there has to be a balance between the consumer demand ceramics and the art ceramics, which is what I really love. I can get bored very quickly.'

Judi's home is a gallery of her work over time. The kitchen features a magnificent tiled breakfast bar complete with ceramic feature pieces from the Clay Art Studio days: wine bottle and glasses, fried egg, knife and fork, and salt and pepper. The black mosaic dresser displays, amongst other things, a clock, a candlestick, vases, and a pair of birds, while the wall is home to some of her cute little ceramic dresses. In the hallway are ceramic shoes, mirrors and jewellery holders and the study walls continue the fashion theme with hats and bikinis, and a range of sculptured children's garments. 'These plaster garments were made for the first Taupo Arts Trail,' says Judi. 'Making the clothes is heart stuff.'

Each year Judi makes a point of creating something new for the Taupo Arts Trail. In 2016 her theme is quirky, bright-coloured miniatures — teapots, candlesticks, vases and flowers. But the project that was capturing her attention most when I visited was a series of children's books about fairies. 'During the *Eclectic Wardrobe Exhibition*, the fairies would borrow the garments and put a magic spell on them to make them smaller so that they could wear them. When they put them back on the wall in the morning, they would accidentally put them back in the wrong place.' Hearing this story, Judi's friend Robin McConnell wrote about it for his grandchildren. He sent it to Judi to share with her grandchildren, which got her thinking about turning it into a special picture book. Collaborating together they are hoping to publish it as the first L'Arté fairy story, using the mosaic living room as the home of the fairies. 'Creating the artwork has been a huge learning curve.'

L'Arté was voted number one café destination in the North Island by Lonely Planet. To get to L'Arté, take the Acacia Bay Road out of Taupo, and turn right at Alice's giant blue chair and lamp.

Bernise Williams
(Ngāti Tūwharetoa)

Taupo

Hūiarau — 100 Hūia

Bernise's story is a testament to the healing power of art and creativity. Coming from what she describes as a very dark place, Bernise has returned home — home to her whānau and the place of her birth, home to the art she loved as a child, and home to her iwi and heritage as curator of Māori taonga at Taupo Museum. Specialising in acrylics, her paintings resonate with the Māori imagery which she holds so dear.

'I feel so blessed to have known and been brought up around my nannies; my two grandmothers and three great-grandmothers. Even though they passed away when I was younger I still remember them well, their cooking, the way they talked, the way they laughed, the smell of the house, their humour, their growlings, their strength, but most of all their unconditional love. This is where my inspiration derives from,' says Bernise.

Bernise's artistic story starts at her nan's house, home of her mother's mother. Being the oldest grandchild and living just over the road from Nan she was a regular visitor. As Nan taught herself to do bone carving, weaving or other crafty things, she taught her grandchildren. 'Nan was a very creative person, she was always showing us how to make things, keeping us busy, I guess, so we wouldn't get bored,' says Bernise. 'I've always loved to draw, starting with animals and then portraits in pen and pencil.'

It wasn't until many years later that Bernise would realise what a gift her Nan had given her in nurturing her love of art. After a relationship ended she struggled on her own with her two children, not realising she was becoming depressed. 'I was so unhappy,' she says. She moved back to Taupo, her family home.

Being around positive people and getting involved in courses boosted her confidence and, feeling happier, she started to draw again. 'I had to ask myself, what is it that would really make me happy? And the answer was to create art. I couldn't stop thinking about an art course that I'd heard about. I really wanted to be a part of it, so I pushed myself to apply and was accepted to Toihoukura, the School of Māori Visual Art and Design in Gisborne. I didn't have much time before the course started so I had to organise myself, and my kids. This felt exciting and a bit scary but I definitely felt like I was being guided in the right direction.

'The course opened up a whole world for me, being exposed to so many artists, and different mediums.' Entering with the idea of doing a one-year diploma, Bernise stayed for five years including one year of workshop practice, where she shared a studio with a couple of others. 'I learnt so much, not just about art but about myself and what I was capable of.'

With each exhibition Bernise's confidence grew as many of her pieces sold. In 2010, Bernise was given the opportunity to travel to the Netherlands with Toi Māori, as an exhibiting artist and as part of a kaupapa waka. Supporting the waka crew, the small group of artists based themselves at the university in Leiden, where Bernise helped to run painting workshops.

Returning to Taupo, Bernise worked at three jobs to make ends meet, while she followed another passion also acquired at Toihoukura, namely tā moko, traditional tattooing. When the job of curator came up at Taupo Museum, Bernise was excited to be working with taonga from her own iwi, something which she describes as spiritually rewarding. 'Many of the taonga, photographs and stories connect with my tūpuna [ancestors]; I'm so humbled to be in this mahi,' she says. 'I've had a few emotional moments working here where I've discovered early newspaper articles and historic photographs of my nannies and koros. Every time it brings a tear to my eye, but in a good way though. I think they're just letting me know they're around me and that I'm safe.'

For a while art took a back seat but Bernise recently got back into it, despite spending much of her spare time studying for her Certificate in Museum Practice through Service IQ. The opportunity came up for Bernise to move into her nan's house, which she is currently renovating. It is clear that this is a very special place for her to live. For the moment the artwork is done on the kitchen table, which is a little tricky as Bernise loves to work with large canvases. 'As soon as I finish renovating my bedroom, I'll make a start on my studio,' she says. Bernise is unlikely to hang much of her own artwork on the studio walls as she says she keeps wanting to fix it or play with it. She acknowledges her tendency to overanalyse things. 'I play music to stop me thinking too much. When I'm not thinking it just flows.'

Bernise's current project is to paint 100 hūia. Having discovered an old box of bird drawings and paintings that had been gifted to the museum, Bernise became fascinated with their shape and their special place in Māori culture. For the time being Bernise is creating smaller works using acrylics and oil sticks to layer up the vibrant colours she loves. 'Artwork has been healing for me; a good way of expressing myself,' she says. 'What's important to me is how my artwork makes people feel, rather than how precise it looks. Colour and composition can be so healing.'

Anna Korver
Tataraimaka, New Plymouth

Chisel in Hand

South of Oakura on the coastal road from New Plymouth is a small settlement called Tataraimaka. It is an area well known for its beaches and hiking tracks. It is also the place that Anna Korver calls home. Anna and her partner, Steve Molloy, rent part of the disused Okato dairy factory, which combines their home, their creative spaces and the Korver Molloy Gallery, including a sculptural park in the garden.

The factory, originally known as the Timaru Creamery, was built in the late nineteenth century, and over the years was used by a number of companies for dairy manufacturing. 'There's a few signs of its previous uses around,' says Anna. 'We get so many people come in who used to work here or use it for various things. They're always so excited to see it being used for a gallery space.'

The extensive, open factory spaces and the covered truck bay provide a perfect venue for Anna to create her large, trademark sculptures, many of which are well over a metre high. She works with a variety of materials including wood and metal, but her favourite medium is natural stone, including marble, granite and andesite.

Anna was introduced to carving at a young age by her father, an amateur wood carver. She continued to develop her love of carving, completing a sculptural major at Ilam School of Fine Arts in Christchurch in 2003. While at

Ilam, her work featured in a group exhibition called *12: Dialogues with Time* at Christchurch's Centre of Contemporary Art. This led to her first commissions.

After completing her degree, Anna created a studio space in the Melt Works. This was followed by time spent as a working artist in both Christchurch and Auckland. When she and Steve attended a sculpture symposium in New Plymouth, they made the decision to settle in Taranaki and, a few months later, found the dairy factory and saw its potential.

To most of us Anna's space, with welders, steel, wood and tools, looks like a bloke's engineering shop. 'I spent a few years without a space of my own to create in. This is an absolute dream. There is an area for woodworking and a separate area for metal work, and the truck bay out the back for the wet stonework,' she says. 'I have a desk where I sketch up ideas, and I can leave stuff out, often working on several pieces at the same time. There's room to make all the ideas I have. I have been known to have forty pieces of work on the go at once.'

Anna's workspace is totally functional, with no alterations made to the building. They've added shelves and workbenches and created a desk area for each artist. Anna also has an assistant who works with her. 'Oriah attended one of my workshops. She has a background in landscape design. We work really well together,' says Anna.

Finished work is transferred to the gallery or the sculpture park. 'There is no shortage of inspiration. The materials and the space are inspirational to me,' says Anna.

Anna is an executive member and tutor for Te Kupenga Stone Sculpture Society in New Plymouth. Her courses are well attended by local and international students, and she is pleased to see a growing number of women in what used to be a predominantly male domain. Many of her pieces explore the role of women in society; the challenges and the obstacles. 'I'm a feminist at heart. I believe in the strength of the feminine. Each series explores a different theme, the tensions and emotions, the form and strength.'

The society's premises are also Anna's creative home when she is working on-large-scale pieces (up to four metres high), which require specialised lifting gear. At the time of speaking with Anna, she was working on a 3.5 by 4-metre-high piece of black granite weighing 10 tonnes. These large works are mostly made for outdoor shows.

Anna's works are tactile pieces that beckon you to run your hands over them. They are sometimes abstract and minimalist, and sometimes deliberately exaggerated and structural with strong feminine curves.

Anna plans her work ahead, balancing commission work with exhibitions and sculpture symposiums. 'I usually average fifteen to twenty exhibitions each year, and usually well over fifty pieces. I love tutoring. It reminds me of how fresh and excited I was when I was first learning. I enjoy passing on my knowledge and expanding the industry.' Anna also writes reviews of the latest tools, letting people know what is out there.

Barbara Valintine
Eltham

Champagne She Cave

Most of the time when I'm travelling and interviewing I make appointments ahead, but every now and then I come across a surprise that I can't resist writing about. Barbara Valintine's champagne 'she cave' was a delightful find in Eltham, 50 kilometres from New Plymouth. Set down a side street, I wouldn't have known about it if it hadn't been for a local shopkeeper pointing it out.

Barbara runs a 'new, retro and vintage' shop appropriately called The Bank. The shop, her home and her 'she cave' are set in an old Bank of New Zealand building dating back to 1916. She and husband Mark have faithfully restored the building, including the manager's residence, to its former glory. Built in a neo-classical style with Corinthian columns framing the entranceway, it is reputed to have cost $4700 to build — the modern-day equivalent being $650,000.

At the time the couple bought the building, it had been used as a workshop for car and motorbike restoration, but Barbara and Mark could see the potential past the grimy walls and mouldy ceilings. Barbara did some research and found a complete set of plans in the local library, then went full-time into the renovation while Mark continued working. There were the usual electrical and plumbing upgrades, but by far the largest amount of time was spent on repainting. Barbara has clearly poured her heart and soul into the property.

'I love restoring,' she says. 'I can see the beauty in it. The building talked to us and told us what to do. I just responded to it. It's like one giant painting in three D. It is architecture, fashion and décor. Actually, it's the carrot to the donkey.'

Barbara and Mark lived in the bank manager's residence during the renovation. Mark's photography skills came in handy as they documented before and after each stage. 'There weren't too many "Oh my God!" moments,' she says. 'All the original features have been kept: the tall pillars, the heart mataī floors, the beautifully moulded plaster ceilings, the outside decorative features and the strongroom, complete with twenty-four-inch reinforced concrete walls and ceiling.' Both the inside and outside are simply breathtaking.

Barbara has always been creative, with her surrealist paintings accepted for the James Wallace Art Awards. Her association with the arts also includes teaching, managing art galleries and running her own antique shop, so it was not surprising that partway through the renovation, Barbara decided to open a 'new, retro and vintage' shop. Barbara was in her element, going to auctions,

and buying stock for the shop, which is just as fascinating as the building. There are beautiful treasures for every room in the house, all artfully displayed. It is without a doubt a 'stop and linger' shop.

There is one new addition to the building. During the renovation Barbara discovered a hidden room above what had been the staff toilets. To Barbara it was irresistible. She found a circular, French Provincial style staircase to provide the access and opened up a wall so that the room overlooks the shop. She then set about decorating it with some of those special pieces that, wouldn't you know it, just hadn't sold!

There is a real sense of the theatrical as you walk up the staircase, where you are greeted by heavy purple velvet drapes complete with gold brocade and tassels. Bought at an auction and then put away in a cupboard for a time, they add a sense of opulence, as does the heavy linen roof frieze imported from Italy, which Barbara says was a bit of a nightmare to put up. At the centre of the frieze is a glass chandelier, to which Barbara has added champagne flutes. Everything has been chosen with care. The Cole and Son wallpaper, complete with arches and monkeys, creates a dramatic background for a cream chaise longue. This was the first piece to take up residence, and has since acquired a cushion with skull and fascinator appliqué made by a local crafter, and a fox fur, which is in remarkably good condition. 'It cost a fortune at an auction,' says Barbara. 'My cat was jealous of it initially, but happily curls up with it now.'

Next to the chaise longue is a table that Barbara has hand-painted, and the essential wine fridge, well, champagne fridge, actually. The original kitchen bench, with 1950s-style 'onyx' Formica, serves as a wet bar, with the shelves above housing her collection of retro French coupe glasses with their characteristic hollow stems. Holding one anatomically appropriately, Barbara laughs and explains, 'The design of the glass was [supposedly] based on the shape of Marie Antoinette's breast.' Beside the bench is a retro resin chair and in the centre a French Louis-style chair sitting on a leopard print floor rug. The curtains have been repurposed from Barbara's house in New Plymouth, and the grilles on the windows, which look so authentic, are repurposed wall art from Spotlight. It is a delightful mix of champagne style, cleverly achieved on a beer budget, or as friends so eloquently put it, 'It's just so high camp!' And what does Barbara use her absolutely gorgeous room for? Why, darling, it's her champagne 'she cave', of course. Anyone for an aperitif?

Heather Rees
Taradale

Accidental Art

Three-and-a-half years ago, Heather and her husband, Bob, packed up their house and Heather's sculptures and paintings in Australia and came to New Zealand. For Bob, a Kiwi, it was a return home. For Heather, it was the start of a whole new journey. They purchased their home in Taradale online and were relieved to find it more than met their expectations when they finally arrived. They had wanted a big workshop, art studio, and space around them. It had to be an arty house to reflect their personalities and passions. The house is built in natural timber and has multiple levels, and wide covered decks. The view to the east looks across Taradale to the Napier coastline, and to the west are views of rolling hills. Inside there is creative use of rimu timber and painted walls, which make excellent display walls for their artwork.

Up the stairs is the open plan kitchen and family room, which leads to a large covered deck and it is here, behind a sculptural driftwood curtain, that Heather has her outdoor or summer studio. Heather is a mixed-media artist, describing herself as a 'chronic collector of junk.' It's a very eclectic mix of junk. Her worktable is covered in springs and pumice, glue and guitar heads, metal pulleys and even a shoe last. Under the table are buckets of driftwood,

and on the deck are two-dimensional sculptures she is working on. 'I love recycled materials: old metals and tools. I love the old look and the patinas,' she says.

Talking about her creative style, she says her inspiration usually comes by accident. 'I just throw things around until something comes of it. I'm really interested in the textures and surfaces of natural and man-made objects together. I like things to look organic. And I try to respond or react to the relationship between the natural world and humankind, and the state of the environment.'

Downstairs Heather has another studio where she paints, and the room doubles as guest accommodation. Bob does all her framing, working with recycled timbers, and also makes her canvas and boards for painting. In Australia, Heather had a purpose-built studio, where she mainly focused on cold encaustic wax, which she builds up in layers.

On returning to New Zealand, one of Bob's goals has been to get more in touch with his Māori heritage. Heather's latest work in acrylics is a series entitled *Be the Bird*. 'It is a reflection of his world and what I see. I like New Zealand motifs.' It was through the Community Arts Napier Gallery that I came to meet Heather, and I was fortunate to see these paintings in the process of being hung. This was Heather's first solo exhibition, showing the versatility and range of her work, from paintings in acrylic to encaustic wax, and two- and three-dimensional sculptures. She says it has been a highlight. 'I'd exhibited in group exhibitions before. Relocating, I needed something to focus on. I have time now.'

The sculptures are made from found pieces. They are an interesting mix of materials, and would fit well in the popular contemporary retro/industrial style. My favourite piece, entitled *Sky Guides*, was a circular, two-dimensional sculpture about Māori navigational skills, featuring a waka, the sun and moon and stars made from old saw blades, and a recycled oak wine barrel lid that reflected the world.

Heather has no plans to slow down her creative flow. 'I'm excited to keep going. I need to do art . . . There's something missing if I don't.' Heather's work can be found at Artmosphere in Waipawa.

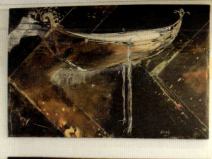

Creating Your Very Own Her Space

A 'Her Space' can come in any shape and size, and can be made on any budget. While everyone dreams of having a purpose-built large space, the women in this book are living proof that any space can work for you, if you set your creative mind to it. If finding a space is an issue, separate your thinking into working space and storage space. While it might be nice for them to share the same space, it just isn't necessary. Sometimes you can create space in a room or garage purely by making better use of that space, going up the walls with storage rather than across the floor. A clean-out of a large cupboard could provide a solution, or asking your grown-up children to store their own belongings might free up space.

Your Workspace

Safety — No matter how big or small your space is, your most important priority is safety. If you are working with chemicals, glues or processes that create heat or unpleasant odours, do it outside with lots of ventilation or install extractor fans if inside. Attend to electrical safety — no overloading multi-boxes — and use isolating transformers if you have to use water around electricity. Watch out for trip hazards, making sure your floor is clear around your worktable, and provide safe storage and usage of tools.

Your worktable — The single most important piece of furniture is the table you work at. It doesn't have to be flash, but it does need to be solid and stable with an easily cleaned top surface. This is followed very closely by your chair, which needs to be set at the right height to provide adequate support. A quick look at any ergonomics website will tell you the appropriate sitting posture for your activity.

Lighting — Daylight is by far the best light to work in. Our eyes like it and it's free, but you may require an adjustable lamp for those close-up jobs. There are some great lights on the market, which also include a magnifying glass. Avoid fluorescent lights and lights shining over your shoulder, which create shadows on your work.

Heating/cooling — None of us do our best work when we're too cold or too hot. Normal household heating and cooling are usually adequate unless you have a process that creates heat. Watch for flammable products, including glues, chemicals, paints and fabrics.

Storage — Over the years you will, if you haven't already, accumulate a significant collection of raw materials, which can amount to many hundreds of dollars. There are many storage solutions to be found within each of the stories, but as an overview here are some things to think about.

As a minimum, storage solutions need to be dry and out of direct sunlight. Some items may require special temperature conditions, particularly anything classified as dangerous goods. Think about safe storage for these items including locking them away from young children. Storage also needs to provide easy access, be an easy place to remember, and be quick to tidy up. Whatever the solution make sure you are disciplined in putting caps on and returning tools to their home, minimising wastage and ensuring years of safe usage. Repurpose furniture, such as filing drawers, dressers, sets of drawers, shelves, crates, large jars, shoe boxes, clothes racks, and pallets or splash out and buy stackable or rollaway plastic bins.

Think also about storing finished work. Nothing is more heartbreaking than spending hours making something, only to have it ruined in a few seconds because it got in the way and was damaged. A great place to store finished works is on the walls or tables in your house for your friends and family to enjoy. It also allows you to stand back and view them from different angles and in different lights. Avoid the temptation to want to keep touching it up or adding something to it. When it's finished and comes out of your workspace, it's finished.

Pinboards — Not necessary but extremely useful to capture ideas, pin up mementos, and save reminders. Create a board or use Blu-Tack to hang things on the wall. Pinterest has some great ideas.

Make it inviting — Imagine your dream space. What draws you to that vision? Is it sunlight, warmth, colour, having a comfy chair, a worktable, having mementos or materials around you? Whatever it is, build it into your space as much as you can. Making your space inviting will encourage you to potter around in it.

Sharing your space — If your space is inviting for you, it may also be inviting to your family and friends. Set ground rules. How do you want them to respect your space and the time you spend in there? Is your space a 'no go' zone, a 'knock and wait to be invited' zone, a 'come in only if the house is on fire' zone, or are you happy for people to come and go? Many of the women in this book have been very specific about their spaces being just for them, their havens. While there are no right or wrong answers, it is probably not helpful to have an 'enter at your own peril' policy, where you may be receptive one day and craving your solitude another day. Discuss it up front so that everyone knows. If you truly are happy to have your children in your space, set aside a corner for them with the things that they are allowed to use.

Susan Mabin
Waiohiki, Hawke's Bay

Set in Concrete

Set behind the craft shop at Waiohiki Arts Village is a huge garage divided into workspaces. It is home to a wide variety of artists, including Susan Mabin, a sculptor, whose preferred medium is concrete. 'I love the texture of it, the abrasiveness of it. You can embed things in it. But it is heavy,' she says.

Susan has only recently started to focus on her art. 'I spent twenty years wanting to do it. Now I can,' she says. While studying for a Bachelor of Visual Art and Design at Eastern Institute of Technology in Taradale, Susan started a body of work entitled *Unhinged*. She completed her degree in 2014 and was named top visual art student. The collection focuses on relationships, power imbalance and emotional abuse. It is confronting, mesmerising and a little disturbing. The sculptures combine ceramic figures with found objects, building materials such as concrete and reinforcing rods, and everyday objects like tables and chairs. In the exhibition introduction Susan describes the work as autobiographical.

'I had a story to tell that I needed to make sense of. As painful and challenging as some of the work was to create, by giving myself permission to explore the issue of domestic abuse (be it emotional, psychological, and/or physical),

and then put it into the public arena, I wanted to raise the awareness of a subject that is rarely talked about, that is often hidden behind the thin veneer of 'home' but is a significant problem facing our society today. The hidden becomes visible. With visibility there is hope for change.'

At the time it was a cathartic release, but Susan says it's not so emotional for her now she has moved on.

Susan's workspace is utilitarian to say the least. Concrete floors and corrugated iron walls. The floor-to-ceiling shelves are filled with an eclectic mix of 'junk' and the tools and materials of her work. There's steelwork and cardboard boxes, wooden frames and netting, blocks of wood and plastic hosing. The range of materials is remarkable.

Initially used for storage while Susan was studying at EIT, this space has now become her creative haven. It's a practical space, and works well for the messiness of working with concrete and plaster. In the hallway another shelf houses her moulds for her ceramics, and chair legs and stools that will be repurposed as part of her sculptures. Using found objects appeals to Sue. 'They carry echoes of the past, which I can then carry over to my new work.' Her kiln, previously packed away, now sits in the corner awaiting Susan's inspiration. She's keen to start using it again after it's been in storage for five years. It holds the remnants of a past project — small ceramic faces. There is a welding set in another corner. 'It [the space] looks messy,' she says, 'but I know where everything is. I love playing around with all the bits and pieces.'

Susan currently works as a practice nurse to pay the bills, but at night and

in the weekends she is an artist who continues to have something to say. 'I like to create work that's commenting on something,' she says. Susan is constantly surrounded by her work, both finished and unfinished, and experiments with combinations of found materials until it feels right. Her current work, which she initially described as 'monuments to the un-monumental', uses concrete and bird's nests in an unusual juxtaposition of the man-made and natural. There must be 30 bird's nests in the space — some natural and some painted in bright fluoro colours — all gathered from local fruit orchards. 'We are full of self-importance, disregarding every other creature,' she says. 'I use bird's nests and/or feathers as a metaphor for nature. The bird's nests can also represent home.' The collection of 12 pieces, which is destined for The Corner Space, a curated art space on Auckland's Karangahape Road, is in varying stages of completion. There is a number of pieces around the walls, including a striking piece with the bird's nest cradled in rusted lengths of steel. On the bench is another bird's nest with fluoro yellow pouring from it. And in the centre of the floor is the beginnings of the next piece — wet concrete in a cardboard box mould, which will form the
base plinth.

    A highlight for Susan was spending three months in 2015 doing a residency in northern Iceland in a small isolated town called Ólafsfjörður. During her time there Susan created an environmental exhibition. Collecting rubbish from the beach she set herself the task of making something from it, in three and two dimensions, and installation works. 'Rubbish. It's everywhere,' she says. 'I want to go to other wild and beautiful places and do the same thing, and collate it all together.' The idea forms the basis of her project for her Masters in Visual Art and Design, which she commenced at the beginning of 2016.

Rhonda Lidgard
Waiohiki, Hawke's Bay

Right Place, Right Time

Rhonda Lidgard's love affair with flax goes back to her twenties when, as part of a team-building exercise for work, she learnt how to make putiputi (flax flowers). She remembers that she wasn't too keen initially, but came away loving it. For years that was all she knew how to do, but once the kids left home, in her words, she 'really got into it', going to courses and learning how to make kete (baskets) and pōtae (hats). 'As my love of weaving grew I decided I didn't want to work any more.'

Having always wanted to have a craft shop, she started one in her single garage at home while working as a psychiatric nurse. Her days were full, nursing during the day and weaving flax after work. It was nothing for a typical day to start at 5am and finish anywhere from 10pm to 1am.

Rhonda was burning the candle at both ends, and then it happened. One Christmas Eve, Rhonda had a brain aneurysm. Luckily, she was standing in the Tauranga Hospital intensive care unit at the time, which she credits with her survival. She has no memory of anything after the aneurysm until 3 January. It was a huge wake-up call.

Looking back she says, 'I was where I was because I didn't look after me.' Her recovery was slow and frustrating. In the early days, she could prepare flax for a few hours in the morning and then she would have to go to bed for the rest of the day. Not long after this, Rhonda met her partner, Chris, also an artist, who works mainly in wood. They moved to Napier and started Two Crafts, developing a word-of-mouth clientele. After spending three years working in a Napier warehouse and living in the rental above, they were approached by the Waiohiki Charitable Trust, who provide workspace at nominal rentals for a variety of artists. The trust was closing down its craft shop and approached Rhonda about taking it over. After doing her research and ensuring the trust matched their current warehouse rent, Rhonda took over the shop. 'I had to do lots of networking — getting on with everybody out here,' she says.

At that stage, Rhonda was an accomplished weaver but she hadn't learnt the tikanga (customs and lore) behind the traditional Māori art form. A course at Te Wānanga o Aotearoa in Hastings enabled Rhonda to connect with the spiritual side of weaving, and built her confidence to move from the more traditional weaving to contemporary styles.

Apart from the picking of the flax, all the preparation takes place behind the craft shop under canvas. One marquee houses the tables for splitting the flax and the other houses the gas burners for boiling it, the dyeing vats, and has additional space for storage. Once dry, the flax is taken into the workroom inside the craft shop. It's a large space, both practical and creative, with a workbench down one side, and a smaller table where Rhonda can work and still see out into the shop.

Although Rhonda enjoys the practical weaving of kete and pōtae, it is artistic weaving that she finds the most creative. 'Having time to play with flax leads you to cover new ground,' says Rhonda. It was a play session that took Rhonda from moulding pōtae to moulding body forms in flax.

Rhonda is frequently asked about teaching, to which she replies, 'I'm not qualified to teach, just come and play with the flax.' She leads a class each week. 'People come and choose what they want to make. It gives people a little taste of it, and reminds me of when I got started.' She cracks a quiet grin. 'Once you're addicted the housework is the first thing to go, and if he's not careful and starts complaining, he's second!'

While there is undoubtedly a wicked sense of humour, there is also a sense of serenity about Rhonda. Perhaps it comes from being grateful for each day. When asked about her future plans she says, 'I think I'm living my dream. I'm where I've wanted to be for a long time.'

Su Hendeles
Whanganui

Alchemy and Magic

Being a photographer myself, I feel comfortable saying most photographers' workspaces are really boring. They consist of a table and a digital computer — not so interesting. So I was delighted to make contact with Su Hendeles, who gives a whole new meaning to the idea of creative photography. Su develops her own photos in a darkroom, but there's no way I could call her 'old school' as she is pushing the boundaries well beyond anything I've seen in modern photography.

Su's approach to photography is best understood by looking at the progression of her work. Her first exhibition, while studying at UCOL in Whanganui, was named *The State of the Art: Marketing Eyesight in the 21st Century*. A practising ophthalmologist, Su focused her lens on the big business of ophthalmological supply, and the shift from treating blinding disease to promoting spectacle-free vision. The photos were relatively standard digital photos, but the installation was not. Wanting to create a third dimension, Su mounted the photos on large light boxes, some of which were old hospital X-ray light boxes.

Her next exhibition was inspired by a German article about the use of fake bus stops to prevent Alzheimer's patients wandering off. Taken with

an infra-red camera and printed as silver gelatin lith prints, the photos have characteristic moody, dark shadows and soft, bright highlights. Su used a jelly lens on the camera to deliberately blur the images, creating a sense that not everything is seen, thus leaving the viewer to complete the unsaid story. 'What really appeals to me [in photography] is what you don't say, rather than what you do say,' says Su.

Lith printing uses a traditional black-and-white development technique, in which the print is grossly over-exposed but the development is slowed down, producing a wide variety of tones, depending on the paper. Every print is unique. This became Su's trademark style, and over the next few exhibitions Su continued to explore both landscapes and portraits, with a range of hues from gritty and harsh black-and-whites to softer delicate warm tones.

Her 2013 exhibition, *Through the Looking Glass*, was inspired by Lewis Carroll, who was also a pioneer photographer. Captured with an 1897 Lancaster Instantograph view camera, on hand-coated silver gelatin, dry plates, this body of work explores a world where nothing is as it should be: upside down, inside out, dream becomes reality, reality a dream. Su explains: 'Historically, photography was reputed to steal your soul. Photography is an act of natural magic, and silver has a special place in its heart. Even in the digital age, souls are not only stolen, but instantly disseminated through cyberspace by means of social media.'

Su, a photographer's daughter, has always had an interest in photography, with her first camera being a Box Brownie, quickly followed by a Contax camera. This interest continued through her medical school years and, when she moved to Whanganui some years later, she studied fine arts at UCOL. 'Everyone was doing art stuff,' she says. 'They were so supportive.' Continuing her studies through the Auckland University of Technology, Su gained her masters, completing a large body of work entitled *Searching for Magic in Dog Town: a Photographic Journey*. 'I made myself go to the most unappealing place I could find. The photographs are made in and around a minor suburban waterway, the Mangaone Stream in Palmerston North. The cameras that created them are lens free, using zone plates to focus light on film. They lack any precise means of adjustment. They are not programmed for perfection by

large corporations. The photographic plates are hand-poured silver gelatin emulsion on glass. This too is an imperfect process. All prints are flawed.'

It is this imperfection and the serendipity of a good shot that fascinates Su. 'It puts the random back into photography. I like that it's sciency. But of course the hardest thing is figuring out where to point the camera.'

What about Su's space? Well, it can be anywhere she can take a photo. A recent project used wet collodion photography so had to be shot close to home, as the plates need to be back in the darkroom before they dry out. Her darkroom is located in Dublin Street in what used to be the Clever Hands shop. She shares this space with her husband, Tom, who converted the galley-shaped darkroom for her. It is a functional space with all the usual trays and chemicals you would associate with a darkroom.

When asked about the challenges of working as a photo artist, she includes the usuals — money, time, inspiration and the tedious work. 'You just have to do it, like washing down twenty-five plates.' She has also found the art world challenging at times. 'The avant-garde can be quite conservative.' But it is clear that Su has many more projects to complete. 'After all,' she quips, 'that's why we have a day job. It pays for the habit.'

Sally Maguire
Waipawa

Artmosphere

On a piece of land in the countryside just north of Waipawa, heading towards Napier, sits a beautifully restored villa, which is the creative home and place of work for Sally Maguire and her partner, Helmut. This villa is home to their gallery, Artmosphere, where the work of about 80 artists is displayed, including Sally's paintings and Helmut's photography.

The story of how the pair met is the stuff that movies are made of. Picture a long beach on a sunny day, Sally walking her dog, Helmut focusing on a shell through his camera lens — all is well with the world. And then the dog runs into Helmut's shot, disturbing his moment, Sally rushes over to apologise, and so begins a commuter relationship that spans the globe from Germany to Waikanae.

After some time in Woodville, Sally and Helmut rescued the villa they now live in from a fire sale — quite literally. If the owners hadn't sold it, they were going to give it to the local fire brigade to use for 'training purposes'.

Moving into it in 2012, they lived amongst the chaos as they renovated. After a year, they opened the gallery with 30 artists. 'The biggest dream of my life was to run a gallery,' says Sally. The setting, both house and garden, is

gorgeous, and the artwork is varied and of a very high standard. Sally is very enthusiastic about her artists, and does a great job promoting their work.

Sitting next to the gallery is Sally's chalet-style studio. Made from timber left over from the renovation, it is a warm, light-filled and inviting space, complete with mezzanine bed accessed by a ladder. A beautiful arched window was given to Sally by friends, and provides an inspiring view of the countryside. A fireplace surround, found boarded up behind some wall panelling in the villa, has been upcycled into a bookshelf.

Sally's brushes sit in three large containers on the windowsill, framed by the view. In another corner of the studio is Sally's paint shelf and in the opposite corner stands a set of drawers. It is simply but endearingly furnished, and a lovely space to be in.

It is here that Sally creates her trademark paintings, for which she has established quite a name. Perhaps unexpectedly, Sally paints cows. 'I'm in love with cows,' she says. 'It started with fence posts,' which still feature in the foreground of some of her work. The posts are layered up in paint to provide a three-dimensional effect. Sally is very specific about which cow she wants to paint and says she will sometimes travel for hours to find the right cow.

Sally also paints on glass, sandwiching the wet paint between two pieces of glass to create a liquid effect. The colours are vibrant and striking, and with the forms softened around the edges they are eye-catching. On the day I interviewed Sally she was painting something quite different: a relic of the past — a car bonnet from a 1930s Ford Prefect. It was stunning.

Sally's favourite escape is Waikaremoana, a place she returns from filled with energy. Sally has an interesting take on energy. 'When you're painting, energy comes through you rather than of you,' she says. 'To be an artist lets your spirit sing.' Sally certainly seems to have boundless energy. As well as painting, she looks after the gallery, which is open seven days a week.

Sally also has another space — a three-storey weatherboard watchtower with 360-degree views. The tower was moved onto a friend's property, where it still resides, in the 1980s after spending its previous life as a forestry watchtower. The interior is original with a bed, a sink, an old dial-up phone, and a potbelly stove. There is no electricity though. It even has the compass markings above the windows. 'It will be my other secret space,' she says, 'where I can create with only the sounds of crickets and birds singing.'

Talking of the future she says she would love to have a solo exhibition, but she keeps selling her works. She is passionate about the environment, and concerned about the loss of New Zealand's forests and wetlands, and the extinction of birds such as the hūia. 'This is the serious side to my painting,' she says. 'I'd like to incorporate the idea of how we can get it back.'

Tracy White
Woodville

At the Crossroads

Woodville is a small rural town set at a crossroads. Travelling from Wellington, you can turn left towards Palmerston North or turn right towards Napier. It's a great stopover, particularly if you are into antiques and collectables. But now I have another reason to stop — Tracy White's shop. It is situated in what used to be the post office, and I found it absolutely intriguing.

I haven't had much experience with wool and natural fibres other than for knitting, so I wasn't sure what I was looking at in many cases or what could be done with it. But I was fascinated by the colour and textures of the wool, silk, alpaca, and rabbit yarns hand-dyed by Tracy for the fibre-artist market. There were brightly coloured packs of carded merino slither ready for spinning or felting, shiny bright yarns of natural silk drying on a clothes rack, and multi-fibre packs in multiple colours, including a lovely combination of muted mulberry and sage green. On another table was a collection of felted fabric pieces with matching yarns and slither, the cutest range of handcrafted buttons and felted flower brooches. There were twisted hanks of spun wool and silk strips, and there were brightly coloured bunches of alpaca locks. Everything was arranged with an artist's eye.

There was also a range of completed products — scarves in silk and felted

merino, knitted hats and slippers, felted bags and my absolute favourite, a hobbit bag. I could easily see that for a fabric artist entering Tracy's shop, must feel like landing in Aladdin's cave. There were so many beautiful things to choose from.

Tracy does all her dyeing at home. She uses mostly commercial dyes, but refuses to dye cotton or linen because of the waste product that goes down the sink. With the wools, the dye is spent so there is no concern around water pollution.

Stepping from the shop into the workroom and storeroom was like stepping into another world. From the order of the showroom to the creative chaos of the workroom is an enormous contrast. Everywhere I looked there was 'stuff'. Books and fleeces, yarn cones and equipment. 'It's not always like this,' says Tracy. 'We just finished a local fibre show, so there is stuff everywhere.' Tracy holds up an S and an N, part of the words 'spin in' she and a group of friends had yarn-bombed specifically for the show. Tracy assures me there is some

order to the storeroom, but I get the feeling you would really have to know your stuff to figure it out.

Tracy does know her stuff though. She has a diploma in textile design. Experimenting with loosely set warp and weft weaving, unspun yarns, felting and screen-printing fabric books, she felt she had found her niche. The difficulty was how to make money from it. Tracy had already decided she didn't want to design for a company. It was just at the time that computer design was being introduced and Tracy felt this was out of her skill set and not how she wanted to design.

In her final year Tracy worked at Rotocard in St Arnaud, gaining industry experience, and was offered a job at the end of it. It was here that Tracy was first exposed to a fibre-craft shop where they were spinning and trialling dyeing and fabrications. Tracy also spent a lot of time in the shearing shed as a wool handler. 'The shearing shed taught me a lot about myself, and to grow a thick skin,' she says.

After spending some time at Lake Rotoroa Tracy made the decision to enrol in a diploma in wool, through Massey University. Tracy describes the course as 'the most informative months of my whole life.' In comparison to the textile design course, the wool diploma was completely factual, from growing the sheep right through to exporting the wool.

After completing the course she was offered a job teaching on the design school programme back in Wellington, once a week for six months. 'It was a good experience,' she says, 'but it scared the pants off me.' It was during this time that Tracy walked into Kirkcaldie & Stains and saw a live merino shearing demonstration. Being in the right place at the right time, she was offered a job by the shearing contractors, a husband and wife team, who worked for Orongorongo Station.

Tracy was delighted to get the opportunity to travel with Tom Dodd and his shearing gang to Norway. 'It was an amazing trip. Most of their shearing gets done in the slaughterhouses. You get up early, shear the sheep, and then they are slaughtered. We also had a weekend in Hardangervidda, affectionately known as the 'Roof of Norway', gathering sheep Heidi style.'

Tracy has also completed a diploma in adult teaching, which she says has been useful for running her classes and the Creative Fibre Group, which meets each week in her backroom. Tracy sells her work in galleries as well as in the shop. She says she finds balancing making money and doing what she wants a challenge. 'In terms of income, it's a no brainer, you'd get a real job.

'It's a lovely way to live,' she says, 'but it's a curse too. I don't have hobbies, there isn't time.'

Sue Lund
Levin

Her Space, Any Place

Walking into Sue Lund's garden in Levin was like opening the gate to a fantasy land. Everywhere I looked there were odd and unusual things to catch the eye. There were mannequins, one under a hairdryer, and another in a hedge with a fishing pole. There was a model duck in the pond, and four ladies' legs holding up a bar, and a car bonnet on the fence. All of these pieces were painted in Sue's trademark style, a vivid kaleidoscope of colour. They were quirky and curious, and left me wanting to investigate what was around the corner. But above all else, the thing I most wanted to do was smile. If art can be humorous, then Sue is one of the stand-up comics of the art world. I'd never seen anything like it before and I simply loved her work.

 Sitting on the deck are Sue's next victims — a huge lion that had been a prop for the *Narnia* films, a pig, and some sheep all awaiting their colours. Sue works in acrylic and resin, starting with a base coat in black, white or red. She then builds up layer upon layer of paint to create the final effect. The detail is incredible.

 Also on Sue's deck are her billboard poems. I am treated to a solo performance of the poem 'Pain . . . t'. Sue's resonant voice reminds me of a female version of Sam Hunt, and there is a lyrical, rhythmical style to her speaking. It is amongst all this amazing creativity that I sit in the sun and begin my interview with Sue.

As the youngest of four children by many years, Sue says she had a more solitary life than most children. She enjoyed being on her own then and says she enjoys the solitary life of an artist now. Sue is practical by nature, and has turned her hand to gardening, sign-writing and waitressing over the years, doing whatever work came to hand as she painted and travelled.

At 25, she enrolled in a fine arts degree at the National Art School in Sydney. 'It was a traditionally structured course, focusing on sculpture and paint, including eight to ten hours of life drawing each week,' she says with a chuckle.

Returning to New Zealand, Sue started working on abstracts, but she describes this time as really difficult. Despite supportive family and friends, Sue started to feel the loneliness, and struggled to deal with the issues her paintings were bringing up.

In 2003, she enrolled in an advanced diploma in formless art through the Learning Connexion. Prior to this Sue had always painted with her piece upright on an easel. The new formless art approach had her working on the ground bent over the picture. 'It pulls you down into the picture,' says Sue. 'You have very little peripheral vision of it.'

Large, layered, dimensional works became Sue's focus. On completion of the course, she was asked to paint one of the Learning Connexion buildings in Wellington, a project that eventually extended over eight years and eight buildings. The buildings reflect Sue's humour featuring feet sticking out of one end and a head out the other. 'My work is bold,' she says. 'To be honest I'm an attention seeker. Notice me. Notice me.'

There is another side to Sue that is deep and spiritual, and she has a number of tales of things that have occurred in the Learning Connexion buildings that leave you wondering. One story involved spilled paint — it was always kingfisher blue that would spill. She'd get it cleaned up, go and buy more, and then there'd be another spill. During this time she was also subjected to a number of kingfisher attacks while she was painting. This continued throughout the painting of the first building until the pōwhiri. After that nothing more happened. Sue believes in synchronicity and that things happen for a reason.

Sue started painting forms, initially mannequins, when she was working at the Learning Connexion and found people kept asking for more of them. The forms extended to horses and elephants — anything she could get her hands on. Sue's garage is full of boxes containing sheep and pigs, her latest artistic

subjects. Just around the back of the shed is a stack of mannequins that is about waist-high, all awaiting her next project.

Anything can fall victim to Sue's artistic whims. The empty paint pots from painting the buildings were flattened and became canvases for her work, as did the paint tubes, which were mounted and resined. Sue sometimes works in oils, usually earthy shades, and she has examples of charcoal paintings in her house.

Sue works when the mood takes her, which is often. She works at night, wanting to catch those moments and ideas, and she loves to work outside on the deck or in the garden or in her shed. It's a typical 1950s double garage where the cars park end-to-end, but the car hasn't had a look in since Sue moved in. In winter she retreats inside to her table by the fire. Like her other work surfaces it is stacked with paints and brushes, and bits and pieces. It's messy, it's chaotic, and it's creative. It's how she likes to work and live.

Moving from Wellington to Levin was about finances, she says. 'I hate that money has to be the driver, but when I get sales it feels good.' Sue sells her work through the Christchurch Art Show, the NZ Art Show in Wellington, and through a select number of galleries. But most of all she loves it when a buyer seeks her out and they can talk face-to-face.

Sue is a fair dinkum Kiwi girl. What you see is what you get, and what you get is deep and humorous, and courageous and caring. 'I feel braver in my paint than in real life sometimes,' she says.

Rachel Pfeffer
Otaki Gorge

Goodbye, Proper Job

I found Rachel and her Totaranui Glass Studio down a tree-lined country road in a small community where everyone knows each other, the kids all go to the local school, and the quiet is filled only by the sounds of birds and insects. It is an incredibly picturesque spot.

For Rachel, her home-based studio is particularly special, as it was her mother's home and pottery studio. Rachel and her husband purchased it 10 years ago, renovating the house and revamping the garden. 'I can feel Mum leaning over me,' she says. 'What have you done to my garden?' I'm sure her mum is pleased as the house, garden and outdoor studio have all become part of a much loved home.

Rachel is the youngest of 10 children, and remembers always being creative. As a six-year-old, she used to walk past a glass artist's workshop and loved looking at the fine glassware and watching the flame work. As an adult she has always sewn, crocheted, and decorated cakes, but they have always been sidelines. 'I couldn't be an artist,' she says. 'I had to have a proper job. I had to be responsible.'

Learning to lead-light rekindled her childhood love of glass. 'I realised I loved

it a great deal.' After many years handling the administration for her husband's automotive business, and lead-lighting as a hobby, Rachel, at age 40, decided 'it was time to do what I wanted.' She moved into her mother's pottery studio, originally a Skyline garage, adding solid worktables to handle the heavy glass, and setting up to make stained glass windows. But she was soon to find that the market was seldom steady. Wanting something that would keep her busy all the time, she developed a range of sculptures incorporating timber and stained glass. 'I had to teach myself woodwork,' she says. 'I would beg information from builder friends, asking "What tool do I need to buy to do this?"'

The carport was eventually converted into a wood workshop, and the courtyard and back room became her display areas. Rachel laughs as she talks about the carport. 'It was built for creative people [her mum]. It wouldn't be right for it to have a car in it! I can still see Mum's potting wheel here, and there's even splashes of glaze on the wall from Mum's days as a potter. It's a very happy place for me.'

The sculptures were, in Rachel's words, phenomenally successful. Three years ago, Rachel opened the studio to the public for the first time. She enjoys being part of the Kapiti Arts Trail. 'It's great to watch and listen to people talk about your art.' A highlight for her was the first time someone stopped her in a shop and said, 'You're that glass artist, aren't you?'

'Every day is a highlight,' says Rachel. 'I love what I do, and I'm very thankful that I'm at a stage where I can do this.' Working as an artist in a home studio is not without its challenges though. Sourcing specific art glass, which is

all imported, can be challenging. She admits to being, in her children's words, a control freak. 'I like to be organised and tidy, and I read the riot act when tools are not where they should be.' More challenging, however, is being on her own. 'Being an artist is a lonely business,' she says. 'Facebook is one of my greatest tools. I can talk to artists around the world, and because I'm not competing with them they are very free with their techniques.'

Rachel's current project is an enormous window, entitled *Tree of Life*, for the local school's newly built hall. She starts each project with a sketch, which, once approved, is scaled up to life size, and then finally turned into a working drawing or 'cartoon'. While she enjoys the commission work, she loves the sculptures and mirrors, where she has free rein. 'It's where my imagination takes me.' Her favourite works are the tall landscapes, which are inspired by and named after the places she's tramped.

Finding time to learn new things is also challenging. Her next steps are to move further into hot glass. Rachel has just bought a giant kiln, and wants to experiment more with flame working, melting and manipulating fine pieces of molten glass. She's not keen on glass blowing, however, something I find entirely understandable. When asked if her husband is supportive she replies, 'Yes. The only diamonds he has to buy are diamond-tipped saw blades.' Most blokes would think that was pretty good.

Paula Coulthard

Rangitumau, Wairarapa

Raising the Flag

With the recent debate over whether New Zealand should have a new flag, Paula Coulthard is definitely working in a topical field. However, her flags are anything but utilitarian in design. They are works of art.

Paula's life as an artist started at the Canterbury School of Fine Arts where she completed her bachelor's degree in sculpture. She went on to work in Auckland making props and costumes for the film and television industry. Her best known film is *The Last Samurai*, for which she was costume props supervisor. When her children were little, Paula moved away from prop making, becoming increasingly concerned about the toxic chemicals she was using.

Paula launched her fashion and homeware label, Coulthard, which used natural fibres such as wool, silk, linen hemp and cotton. The label was well received in the competitive clothing industry, winning the urban streetwear category at the Pasifika Awards two years running. The awards sponsored her into New Zealand Fashion Week with a nautical showing, including garments made in her trademark, Kiwi-inspired vintage fabrics. Speaking of the fashion work she says, 'I wasn't trained in it. I just fell into it. It evolved into one-off pieces.'

Collaborating with Ursula Dixon, the pair decided they would like to go to WOW (World of Wearable Arts), and that it would be fun to have something in the show. They entered the 2007 WOW with a piece entitled *Rattle Your Dags*. Both Ursula and Paula came from rural areas, and wanted to create something that reflected their upbringings in sheep country, and their pride in their country roots. The idea crystallised when Ursula saw a stack of wool sacks on the side of the road. The sacks were unfortunately gone when they returned, but they were able to source some second-hand, and set about boiling them to remove the sheep muck and oil. The markings, however, remained.

Rattle Your Dags took six weeks to complete, with a headpiece made from a BMX helmet to which they attached a set of curly merino horns. The body of the garment was a corset with leg-of-mutton sleeves, and the pants were made with layer upon layer of wool. And, of course, there were the dags, made from hemp rope and crystal so they would sparkle as the model moved. Their entry won the South Pacific section, the first-time entrant section, and then took out the supreme award. In 2008 they entered again, with *Loaded*, which was runner-up in the open section.

The year 2008 was a big one for Paula, as she teamed up with Sue Haldane of The Boiler Room, a label that restored and redesigned furniture. Together they formed a furniture-making company with the brand Union, creating one-off designs using items many would consider junk — something that was ground-breaking at the time. Paula is quoted in the *New Zealand Herald* as saying: 'The stuff that's 100 years old is still

around because it is so good. I love the story of what its life has been. There's a romantic idea of what it's seen and the past. I like things that are a little aged. I don't like them bright, shiny and new.'

It was in Aratoi Wairarapa Museum of Art and History in Masterton that I was to find Paula's latest work — her flags. These led me to visit her home-based studio. After many years living in Auckland, Paula and husband, Simon, a writer for radio and an arborist, decided it was time to escape the rat race. 'We'd been doing the same thing for the last ten years . . . we wanted a bit more land . . . and we wanted a change of lifestyle before we got too old to do it,' Paula explains.

While visiting Paula's aunt in the Wairarapa, they found their dream block of land within a week and thought 'Why not here?' They gave their architect what Paula described as a very airy-fairy brief, saying 'We want a playground of a house, an adventure where you don't know where everything is or where the hallway leads.'

Paula's studio is a loft over the kitchen area, with sloping timber walls and a view to die for out over the surrounding rolling hills. It's light and airy with a warm ambience provided by the natural timber finishes. Despite its relatively small footprint, the loft feels very spacious. There is space for fabric storage to one side and a bench with books, paints and the usual artistic paraphernalia on the other side. In the centre of the room is a stand-up worktable where Paula creates her large (up to two metre) flags. Paula uses jute or cotton canvas, which she stone washes or ages to provide the desired finish and drape. There is a real vintage feel to the flags despite the fact they are made from new materials. 'I like doing the aging and treatments of the flags,' she says.

Downstairs from the loft area is Paula's office, creating a distinct separation between the business and creative zones of her work. The two areas are connected by an ingenious set of stairs that double as drawers.

The images on Paula's flags are inspired by iconic New Zealand scenes such as Aoraki/Mt Cook and Rangitoto Island. These are painted onto the fabric using stencils that Paula also creates. Each flag is a one-off. A variety of ensigns can be used in the upper left corner, although the most commonly chosen are the Union Jack, with the Southern Cross stars often forming part of the overall design. Paula's work can be seen in The Poi Room in Auckland and Aratoi in Masterton. Much of her work is by commission, with flags being sold in New Zealand and internationally. Speaking of her flags she says, 'They are an object, even though they are a painting and go on the wall. That suits me. Basically I'm a sculptor rather than a painter.'

Anthea Crozier

Masterton

A Doll's House for Adults

Anthea Crozier's garden is as pretty as a picture with a hint of yesteryear: beautiful roses, mature English trees, colourful flowers and lush, green lawn, with the tranquil sound of a small stream at the end of the garden. It would make a beautiful painting, which is appropriate as Anthea is a watercolour artist. With her meticulous eye for detail, she envisioned her perfect studio — a curved roof, a red stable door in two halves, red wheels and lots of natural light. Yes, Anthea's studio is a caravan. Although Anthea has lived in many parts of the world including Africa, Asia and South America, it was the classic English shepherd's hut that inspired her choice of studio, which sits in her garden as though it has always been there.

Because of access difficulties, Anthea contracted a local company to build the caravan on site. Measuring just 10 square metres, it feels surprisingly spacious as sunlight streams through its white-painted French doors. In the corner is a wooden tea trolley, which serves as Anthea's artist's station with easel and paints. On the opposite wall is a mirror so that Anthea can see a painting as a whole rather than the detailed parts she's been working on.

'It's the right brain/left brain thing. It shows up the mistakes,' she explains.

Opposite the French doors is a table and chair, which beg you to sit down and have a cup of tea. Beside the stable door, located at the rear of the caravan, is a bookshelf, and the final piece of furniture is a visitor's chair, the most frequent user of which is the cat or dog who stroll in and out with full ownership rights to the space. When asked what the appeal of her caravan is, Anthea says, 'It's a doll's house for adults. I leave the phone behind. It's a really nice space to be in.'

Anthea says she has always painted and drawn. While working on her degree in zoology, Anthea did a lot of technical drawing, which proved useful

when living in Peru where she created illustrations of local potato varieties. Coming to New Zealand on holiday, Anthea and her husband ended up staying, buying a sheep farm, and farming until 10 years ago when she retired into town. Having always lived a busy, productive life, first teaching and then farming, Anthea says, 'It took five years to give myself permission to paint. There was always the "have to do" things which took priority.' Once she started she didn't look back. 'The best thing when I retired was I could paint every day. I did it so often so I could improve.

'Drawing is peaceful, watercolour is exciting,' she says. 'With watercolour you decide what you want to do and then hold your breath hoping the paints

co-operate. Watercolour is always challenging because you use water to carry the pigments. Some pigments react differently to others. Earth colours made from oxide bases are heavy pigments and don't move across the page, compared to the newer petroleum-based colours, which scoot across the paper, surprising you in good and bad ways.'

At the time of our meeting, Anthea had just returned from a watercolour-painting course in Whangaparaoa, just out of Auckland. With few other watercolour artists in her local area, Anthea has invested in a painting course each year to learn and get creative support. She has attended courses in Australia and in France. The paintings from these periods reflect the local colour palettes and provide pleasant reminders of the local landscapes.

At her first workshop, American watercolourist Charles Reid demonstrated a technique, painting it and writing instructions alongside. Anthea had it framed and it hangs just inside the doorway of her studio. She doesn't have her own artwork up. 'It's too distracting,' she says.

Anthea says she has always been a visual. The walls and shelves of her home are full of treasures all artfully and mindfully displayed. 'I like gardening

and I like arranging things. Although these days if something comes in, something has to go.' This doesn't apply to art supplies though. 'I collect paints and brushes. I use six paints regularly, and twelve on a lesser basis, but I can always be tempted by something new. You never know when you might need it.'

For Anthea each day brings an excitement and anticipation of what she might paint. It adds the twinkle to her eye and gives her a zest for living. She is finally doing what she most wants to do without any feeling of guilt. 'I just want to paint. I don't beat myself up about it.'

Jan Kerr
Raumati South

Wearable Art to Art to Wear

Postage stamps and wine-bottle labels are an odd combination in anyone's books, but they are just two of the many places where Jan Kerr's World of Wearable Arts (WOW) designs can be found. Jan has entered WOW 13 times and, far from being unlucky number 13, her 2011 entry, entitled *Hermecea*, won both the Weta award for the garment that best crosses the boundaries of film and wearable art, and the open section award. This was not the first of Jan's entries to win prizes. She has won numerous awards including two awards for creative excellence, and a runner-up to the supreme award.

   Hermecea was chosen by Brancott Estate Wines to grace their limited edition, collectable, Sauvignon Blanc bottles. This striking work was inspired by hermit crabs. Jan describes them as 'shy, little creatures', something she says she can relate to in her own life. Using a shell as a guide, Jan started by creating the collar, twisting recycled copper wire to get the shape. She then moved on to the helmet, creating all the spikes by hand. *Hermecea* comes complete with a fully functional tail, which mimics the movement of a lobster tail. Texture is given to the jacket by machine embroidery, hand-painting and more spikes. It took two years to complete, and when finished took up so much room that it left a big void in the house when it was gone. *Hermecea* is now part of the permanent WOW collection, which is touring the world.

Just days prior to winning with *Hermecea*, Jan was offered a job by Richard Taylor at Weta Workshop. At the time, she was gallery manager for Raumati's Lush Gallery. Describing the offer as a huge opportunity, she says, 'It didn't seem real. I worked really hard for years and suddenly it was acknowledged.' Jan spent three months working four days a week on costumes for the orcs in *The Hobbit*.

Another of Jan's creations, *Cailleach Na Mara (Sea Witch)*, was chosen by New Zealand Post to feature on a stamp to commemorate the World of Wearable Arts in 2004. This was Jan's fourth entry, which received a highly commended in the 2001 Oceania Section. Pictured on the $2 stamp, the 'bag lady from the sea' is made from recycled materials, as are many of Jan's creations. It incorporated papier-mâché sea creatures, lace, beads, driftwood, bones and shells caught up in a fishing net.

Jan's costumes have frequently made the news. Her paua-inspired 2002 entry, *Quintessentially New Zealand*, created quite a stir when it was modelled by Helen Clark at a Tourism New Zealand showcase in Sydney. It wasn't the norm for prime ministers to arrive at foreign meetings in fancy dress.

All of Jan's creations start life in the living area of her Raumati South home. Jan doesn't have a separate space to work in, preferring to be surrounded by her work. 'I live what I do,' she says.

Her dining table has long since been taken over by her sewing machines. Above the table is a photo gallery of her children and grandchildren, and to one side is a dressmaker's dummy. A favourite spot to work is the couch, where she has lots of bits and pieces tucked away. The messy stuff, like her dyeing, gets done outside in the shed. When I met her, Jan was working on the hand for *The Guardian of the Sea*, a mermaid-based sculpture.

Talking about her creative process, Jan says she is inspired by nature, particularly the coastal area where she lives. I was surprised

when Jan said she didn't start with drawings. 'Drawing is frustrating. I can't draw what I see in my mind,' she says. Instead Jan sees it in her head and writes down lots of words as memory joggers. 'But they always morph along the way.'

Jan's interest in wearable arts and sculpture started when she was living in the Wairarapa, where she attended a course entitled 'Art, Fibre and Design', led by Heather Bush. It was Heather that took the class to WOW and sparked Jan's new love affair, but with five young boys at home there was little time for her artwork.

Jan's first entry into WOW was in collaboration with a friend, and was not accepted. 'It had too much detail and not enough stage presence,' she says. 'I decided to have a go on my own, starting small in the Bizarre Bra section. That was the catalyst to not hold back and go completely over the top.'

Jan also continued her studies, doing a block course with Donna Demente at Whitireia Community Polytechnic.

During her wearable arts time, Jan also worked on smaller pieces, often

focusing on the feminine form. She is now concentrating on these smaller pieces, which she sells through galleries and markets. They are quirky, humorous and thought provoking. Jan's house had many such pieces when I visited: some are keepers, some just there until they are sold. 'The lack of money to buy materials is challenging,' she says, 'and getting your stuff out there. New Zealanders are not as used to three-D art.'

Fortunately, Jan's reputation has seen her winning commissions both in New Zealand and overseas, and her sculptures are in demand. 'I enjoy all my pieces,' she says, 'but I don't have them for long.'

Jan's latest direction is recycling clothing, and working with overdyeing to create 'art clothes to wear' as opposed to wearable art. This fits with Jan's love of creating something out of nothing. Preferring to work with natural fabrics, Jan frequents local op shops, and is often given fabric by friends. Jan says she can't wait to get out of bed in the morning, and she frequently gets ideas in the middle of the night. 'It's just who I am. I can't separate myself from it.'

The M words — Marketing and Money

If you are serious about turning your creative hobby into a business, it's time to talk about money and marketing: who's going to buy your work, how much will they pay and will it pay the bills? You also need to ask yourself: are you ready to work really hard for as long as it takes (which could be years), can you cope without having a steady income, and do you have sufficient savings to cover your start-up costs?

Marketing

Imagine your potential customers. Who are they? How old are they? Where do they live? Do they have discretionary income? Are they happy to pay a premium for handmade, green, sustainable, unique, zany, or on-trend work? Can you tweak your product to provide something special that can carry a premium on the price tag? Identifying potential customers will provide you with valuable information about what to create, where to market your work, and what price you can expect to charge.

You're going to need a business name. Check that your chosen name is available by doing a Google search. Check the company register and search for trademarks. For a website, check that the domain name is available. If it is, then purchase the name immediately, even if you are not going to be setting up a website straight away.

If you've been giving your work away or selling it at a nominal rate then you know there's a market for it, however small. Have confidence that people will buy your work.

Listen to what people are saying about your work. Have a thick skin if necessary. There can be a significant difference between making what people want to buy and selling what you want to make. If you're going to make money, you may have to compromise between making bread-and-butter pieces for which there is larger consumer demand, and making niche, specialist works that make your creative heart sing.

Don't be afraid to put a value on your work. If you don't value your work, you can't expect others to. But be realistic about the price. Check out what others are charging.

Think about multiple price points. Have some bread-and-butter lines, which you can reproduce easily. These will help finance the bigger, more expensive works. If you are at a market, check out what the price points are at similar stalls that seem to be doing good business.

Can you extend or use your work in a different way? For example, photos and artwork for cards, calendars, and home furnishings. Textile works become craft kits. Can you create kits for kids? (This is a huge market.) Can you package your raw materials for resale?

Can you license your designs to someone who will use them in other ways? You get paid a royalty for each time your design is used. This particularly applies to anything that can be photographed and reprinted, and also to patterns. Make sure you get legal advice if you are signing contracts.

Every piece of work, and I repeat *every* piece of work, should have your name and contact details on the item if possible, or on a card attached to it. People can't commission you to create something for them if they can't contact you. There are many artists I would have included in this book if only I had been able to contact them. (Galleries are not always keen to give out details.) Handwritten cards are okay, but a printed card says you're in business and looks professional.

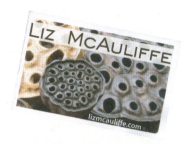

Try different marketing channels: markets, galleries, sale-on-behalf in coffee shops, co-operative shops with other creative people, pop-up shops, and selling online are all good options.

Use social media: websites, blogs, Facebook, Twitter. If you are not computer savvy ask your nearest teenager to help you or, better still, if you can afford it, pay someone to set one up professionally. Think global — the world is your market.

Approach your local gallery. Don't be concerned if they turn you away. On my road trips, I found many galleries did not stock local artists. It's a bit like travelling overseas before you've seen New Zealand. For some of them, artists from further afield seemed more exciting. Other galleries were fantastic at promoting local artists so shop around. Gallery listings for each area can be found online on artfind.co.nz or zeroland.co.nz. Also check out the 'Working with a Gallery' section on page 243.

Try somewhere like Craft World at Westgate in Auckland or NZique in Petone. They have small booths that you can rent and display your work in. There are also similar marketing sites online, for example artofthisworld.co.nz, kiwiartz.com, and felt.co.nz.

Work towards the big retail selling times: Valentine's Day, Mother's Day and Father's Day, and Christmas. Tailor your range for the appropriate time of year.

If you are regularly attending markets, try to have something different each time. Give your customers (and potential customers) reason to keep checking out what you are creating.

Enter competitions. Prize money can pay for your next work and competitions help get your name out there in newspapers, and local and national newsletters.

Holding an exhibition may provide exposure. Check out group exhibitions at local galleries, and art/craft societies. Maybe you're ready for a solo exhibition. This will take planning and dedication, as you will need to have a substantial body of work. When exhibiting, make sure you have an artist profile on the wall and preferably a pamphlet with your contact details for viewers to take away.

Apply for grants, scholarships and residencies. Someone has to get them so why not you? Make sure you adhere to the requirements. Creative New Zealand and community arts groups have money specifically set aside for this each year.

Check out The Big Idea website (www.thebigidea.nz). This is the go-to creative opportunities website in New Zealand for both visual and performing arts. There are job opportunities, both paid and unpaid, commissions, grants, scholarships and exhibition opportunities. There are also media releases and upcoming events, plus you can place a profile in their 'View My Profile' section or upload work into their showcase section.

Check out local information centres for clubs, societies, and groups.

If you are lucky enough to be commissioned to create something, check out the payment terms. When will you be paid? Can you get upfront or work-in-progress payments? For all other sales, gallery arrangements excluded, customers should be paying cash on delivery. Be strong. No payment, no delivery.

Money Matters

Turning your creative 'hobby' into a business is a serious step. You will need to keep financial records and you will need to complete an annual tax return. Make sure you get good financial advice, but above all, before you quit the day job, do your homework and be sure that you have a good chance of making it work. There are no certainties, but this is not the time for dreaming. You need to do some serious financial planning.

Many creatives can find the business end a little overwhelming. Don't be put off by this. Start by committing yourself to learning how to run a business. Go to a course, read a book, and learn to speak the language of money. What is income? What are expenses? How will I know if I'm making a profit? Do I need to open a special bank account? Do I need to register for GST? What do I have to put aside for tax and ACC?

Making a profit is about getting the maths right. You have to sell more, in dollar value, than you spend. Sales less expenses equals profit.

A smart strategy when starting out is to minimise your expenses as much as you can. Watch out for what accountants call overheads. These are things you have to pay regardless of whether you are making creative work or selling anything. For example, if you open a shop you have to pay rent, power and phone, or if you employ staff, you have to pay wages. Regardless of whether you create anything this week or sell anything you still have to pay these expenses. These can also be long-term commitments locking you into payments for months or years. Other overheads can be vehicle expenses, bank charges, accounting and legal fees.

The other type of expenses are variable expenses. They include the raw materials you need to make your product, for example, clay, fabric, paint, and consumables like paint brushes and packaging materials. Shop around to get the best price you can but be careful about bulk buying. It may get you a lower price but having lots of stock does not increase your profit, and may leave you short of cash to pay other bills. Buy only what you can use within a three-month period, less if you can still negotiate a good price. Also watch for freight costs, which may be added to the raw material price. Don't forget to look after your stock. Make sure items like paints, powders and glue are kept dry and resealed after use, and fabrics and trims are stored away from sunlight.

You may also need to buy plant and equipment. There is always a huge range of models available, at a variety of prices. If you are just starting out, you may be able to lease it, but watch that you don't get locked into long-term leases. If you do decide to lease, it will be one of those overheads we talked about. If you are purchasing outright, check what is available second-hand. There are lots of crafters who start out with good intentions but for a variety of reasons don't continue to use equipment they have purchased. Be careful about buying machinery you have not seen working, and check out what maintenance has been done. Buying new is safer but you will pay a premium for your peace of mind.

If you are running a business, you are responsible for keeping financial records. Open a specific business account. Bank all your sales into it and pay all your expenses from it. If you have to use some of your savings to pay for something, transfer the savings into the business account and then pay for the item through the business account. Pay yourself a salary from the business account. Do not pay for personal items from your business account. At the end of each month, take the time to check out whether you have made a profit. If you have expenses, which you pay only once a year, for example insurance, add a twelfth of the cost into your expenses each month when you are working out your profit figure.

Spend time every week working 'on' your business as well as 'in' it. By working 'in' your business, I mean making your creative work. By working 'on' your business, I mean looking after the marketing and the financials, looking at how to grow your business and improve your profits. There are only two ways to increase your profits: increase your sales by either increasing the volume or value of what you are selling, or reduce your costs. Will your orders increase if you ring customers on a regular basis? Which items are selling? Which items are slow? Do you need to expand your range, attend more markets, or place more work with galleries? And keep looking out for commissions, exhibitions and competitions, which can keep you in the public eye.

I will end with the same advice I gave at the beginning. Going into business is a serious step. Get good advice, do some serious financial planning and upskill yourself in managing a small business.

Government Resources and Assistance

There are a number of government programmes aimed at assisting people into business. These include training programmes, advice and financial assistance. They also have valuable information on their websites. Check out the following:

- The Ministry of Business, Innovation and Employment website, business.govt.nz, provides free resources, tools and information to help you start, manage and grow your business, including research and development grants and mentorship. They also have a Biz Information Service freephone number: 0800 424 946.
- Te Puni Kōkiri has a business advice and mentoring service for Māori in business.

- Most local councils have a small business development unit. They are good places for advice and to find out about local courses.
- Inland Revenue has a Small Business Advisory Service to answer questions about tax.
- Work and Income run a training programme 'Be Your Own Boss' for people wanting to start a business.
- If you are receiving a benefit, you may be eligible for Work and Income's flexi-wage self-employment programme. They have two forms of assistance: a short-term allowance to help with costs while you are getting your business started, and a one-off lump sum payment to help with set-up costs such as plant and equipment or purchasing your first stock of raw materials. They also have business training and advice grants, which can help with costs for training in management, marketing, time management and customer service. Be sure to check how any assistance might affect your benefit payments.

Pamela Meekings-Stewart
Pukerua Bay

Grove of the Summer Stars

When Pamela Meekings-Stewart was looking for her 'little piece of paradise' she had a list of non-negotiables: it had to be within commuting distance to Wellington; it had to have a view of the sea; it had to have native bush; it had to have pure spring water; and it must not have any power pylons. Pamela was looking for a space to relax in, a place that she could get away from the busy and stressful life of being a television producer.

It took three years to find the perfect spot, tucked away down a long driveway in Pukerua Bay. She describes viewing the property for the first time. 'I got out of the agent's car to open the gate. When I stepped on to the land it sang to me. I knew it was the right place even though I hadn't yet viewed it.'

Just as Pamela was completing the purchase, she was made redundant when, without warning, TVNZ axed their documentary and drama departments. 'It was a bit daunting just before Christmas,' she says. But she duly went ahead with the purchase and became the proud owner of The Woolshed, a farm of 55 hectares, of which 16 hectares are in natural bush including stands of rare kohekohe trees. Pamela converted the shearing shed into a house, hence the name of the property. The woolshed was divided into a space for two bedrooms, a kitchen and a bathroom, with the rest of the considerable space left open plan.

Pamela has an extensive CV of television, video and film accomplishments, having worked for the Canadian Broadcasting Corporation before returning to New Zealand. Working for TVNZ she was a producer for *On Camera, This Afternoon* and *Today at One*. She lists having worked on more than 50 New Zealand documentaries, and she also produced and directed the award-winning *Pioneer Women* series.

It was while working at TVNZ she started to explore her spiritual side. Raised as a Presbyterian, she moved away from the church and focused on Hindu Siddha yoga. This was to last for 20 years until Pamela again found herself becoming uncomfortable with being told what to do or not to do. Pamela believes strongly in what she calls the 'mystery', something magical beyond the temporal world. 'It informs us, but is not separate from us,' she explains.

A friend encouraged her to go to a Druid workshop in Auckland. 'I was home,' she said.

In 2000 Pamela started The Grove of the Summer Stars, a Wellington Druid group. The group started small and has gradually increased, meeting on each of the solstices, equinoxes, and the four quarter festivals — Imbolc, Beltane, Lughnasadh and Samhain. When the weather is inclement, the group meets upstairs in The Woolshed, which now also hosts a library space open to members.

'There are lots of misconceptions about Druidry,' Pamela says. 'There are three basic tenets: love and respect for the spirit in nature, the spirit in one another, and the spirit in oneself. In our order we have people of Christian, Hindu and Jewish faiths, as well as pagan. We live in harmony with the cycles of nature and celebrate the seasons.'

Alongside Pamela's increasing involvement in Druidry, she continued to work in the film industry. Pamela teamed up to create Pinnacle Producing Ltd, which produced the shows *For Art's Sake* and *The Write Stuff*. She became in demand as an educator in the industry and then branched out into making videos for businesses. She also worked as a management consultant, and served on a number of boards and committees, including NZ on Air and the New Zealand Broadcasting School.

Pamela became sought after for specialised workshops for the development of women in business and in life coaching. This spurred her on to start a women's forum within the Druid group. Meeting on the full moon, the purpose of the group is to explore 'The Divine Feminine' (female spirituality) and to empower women. 'We practise deep listening in our talking circle,' she says. 'Everyone gets truly heard. We support, we don't rescue. If we rescue, we disempower you. If we listen, we empower you.'

When the piles of The Woolshed needed replacing, Pamela raised the floor adding a storey below. This provided a meditation space, a massage room and a meeting space. Pamela also built two retreat cabins. 'The space is welcoming,' says Pamela. 'It has a spiritual energy.' Pamela and her daughter Verity offer a range of services including retreats, pampering sessions, natural therapies, one-on-one counselling, and business or interest group workshops.

Pamela is also a marriage celebrant, something she says gives her a great deal of pleasure.

When asked about living in a public space, Pamela says, 'Since being self-employed, I have never differentiated between work and play. I have my own office and a sleeping platform above.' At one stage she set up one of the cabins for writing, but says she lasted only three days. 'It wasn't working for me. It was too removed.'

Pamela has a love of things that are natural, not neat. She likes being on the west coast and says that when she is stuck in her writing she paces up and down, looking at the view. Her plans for the future include finishing her next book, entitled *Journey of the Thirteen Moons*. 'I also have a novel in the bottom drawer. I take it out and talk to it sometimes.'

Most important of all for Pamela is to continue building a community of like-minded people. 'There is such a hunger in society for community that has a spiritual base to it,' she says. She'd also like to create a community of sustainable eco-housing, saying, 'It will happen if it happens.'

When asked about challenges, she says, 'I've needed to learn a lot about myself. Having been a director, I have had to learn to let go and let others take responsibility. My role now is of a Modron [similar to a matriarch], to support people to find their own empowerment.'

Annie Collins, Vaune Mason, Gemma Miller, Natalie Salisbury

Wellington

The Makers

When Annie Collins and Vaune Mason finished studying at Whitireia, they were keen to turn their artisan jewellery-making skills into a full-time, sustainable business. As for many businesses, their start-up costs were high. There was a lot of different equipment required for jewellery making and very little of it was available second-hand. To buy it brand new was, in many cases, prohibitively expensive. To offset these costs, they came up with an ingenious plan.

Situated in the beautiful old Toi Pōneke building in central Wellington, Annie and Vaune have a unique business model — they rent workshop space and provide tuition in jewellery making for others, as well as making their own jewellery for sale. Their workshop is a large area with space for up to 15 jeweller's desks. These desks can be hired to hobbyists or serious jewellers, on a casual basis or for full-time rental. With the hire fee comes the use of all the equipment and the bonus of having other jewellers around to lend a hand when necessary. 'It works a bit like a gym membership, and is also reminiscent of the old apprenticeship way of working, where experienced artisans trained newcomers by working alongside them,' says Vaune. Annie and Vaune run courses and often continue in a mentorship role when students hire a space. Both see tutoring as a valuable springboard for their own work. 'It works because we are team players. It's like being part of a family, sharing ideas and getting support.'

The workspace is light and airy, with high ceilings and tall windows. For a creative space it is well organised, with everything in its place, including instruction cards to assist with the correct use of the tools.

In addition to their main workspace they also have a machine room down the hallway, which houses lathes, drills and heavier equipment. A recent addition, this space is for messy work and noisy machinery for the likes of woodworking and stone carving.

Annie and Vaune have been involved in many creative enterprises. Highlights include *Shine*, a catwalk, contemporary jewellery exhibition, involving models and aerial artists. *Jewels for Christmas* and *Monster Burlesque* were another two shows that demonstrated their innovative approach to marketing their products.

On the morning I visited, Annie and Vaune were joined by Gemma and Natalie who both rent a space within the workshop on a full-time basis. In order to capitalise on the Christmas market and provide themselves with their own platform from which to sell, the foursome had created a shop on the same premises entitled The Makers. Initially a pop-up shop, it has now become a permanent fixture. Their work is displayed in beautiful rimu display cases alongside curio collectables such as a vintage typewriter, antlers and horns. 'The artisan jewellery market is small and incredibly competitive,' says Vaune. 'As an artisan jeweller you're too niche for some areas of work and too commercial for others'.

Each member of the group has a different style of jewellery. Vaune's designs are the most eclectic of the group, featuring a variety of carved work, folklore, animals and references to nature. Nicknamed the 'commission queen', Vaune also makes a lot of engagement and wedding rings. A favourite project was for three sisters who brought in rings that had belonged to their grandmother, their mother and their stepfather. They asked Vaune to make new rings for each of them from these family heirlooms.

Annie manufactures under the name Buster Collins, and also makes wedding rings to order. Her earrings and necklaces often feature turned wood. Both she and Vaune like to sketch their work before creating it.

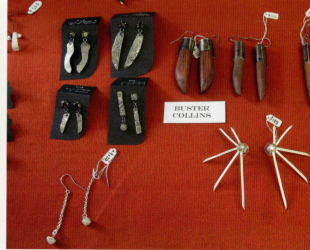

Natalie has two collections: a delicate lace collection with detailed floral patterning, and a briar collection, which focuses on the branches and flowers within the lace design. Natalie prefers to make three-dimensional models rather than sketches prior to manufacture, and refers to computer specific applications if a particularly detailed pattern is part of the design.

Gemma has a different range again: she has created a popular range of life-size roses, crafted in copper and brass. She also upcycles coins and teaspoon handles into a variety of stylised rings, including stones like labradorite. Gemma makes technical drawings as she goes so that she can recreate her pieces.

All of The Makers express their concerns about mining practices and try to use only ethically mined stones. Their silver supplier sources 80 per cent of their silver through recycling. 'It's about standing up for what you believe,' says Vaune.

When asked about the future the group is quick to respond with dreams and plans: an outdoor space to do 'volcano' casting and forging, a studio by the beach, owning a gallery space, and being the 'go to' place for artisan jewellery in Wellington. They hope to be able to market their work overseas. They have found Facebook a good marketing tool, and have also used it to put them in touch with other artisan jewellers around the world.

The Makers are an incredibly talented group of people, and yet there is no artistic rivalry; in fact, quite the reverse. There is a 'collective' mindset; they actively support and encourage each other, and there is a genuine sharing of ideas and encouragement of each other's success. Their creative and innovative approach to their work is inspiring, both from a structural point of view and from their willingness to explore new ways of marketing jewellery. These factors are undoubtedly the secret to their ongoing success.

Jane Brimblecombe
Wellington

In the Quartermaster's Store

There are no cats or rats in this quartermaster's store. There is, however, an abundance of history, a whisper of the sea and a lovely sense of peaceful purpose. Jane Brimblecombe's studio in Wellington's Shelly Bay is part of what is now known as Shed 8 of the Propeller Studios building.

The site started life as part of a military base — the Submarine Mining Depot barracks — in 1887. Munitions stores were added in 1914, and in 1942 major land reclamation allowed space for wharfs, personnel quarters, workshops, a small hospital, and the stores, including the quartermaster's and tailor's stores that now form Jane's workspace.

In 1946, the navy base was transferred to the air force, and was still operational when Jane moved in, in 1996. She told me a great story about finding a very large piece of driftwood that she and a friend rescued from the tide, which almost laps at her door. Together they managed to drag it onto the beach, but it was too heavy to carry home. Enter the RNZAF staff with a tractor and the treasured log was dropped off at Jane's studio, despite air force rules

of non-fraternisation. The RNZAF ensign was finally lowered in 1995 and a large artistic and creative community moved in.

In 2009 ownership was taken over by Taranaki Whānui ki Te Upoko o Te Ika as part of a Treaty of Waitangi settlement. The creative community is no longer as large as it was in its heyday in the late 1990s but a number of artists, including Jane, still choose this historic spot as their base. While the buildings are functional, they have seen better days so many ideas are being floated for their redevelopment in the future. In the meantime, Jane says she loves working here, creating her unique mosaic mirror artworks. In the time that she has leased the building she has moved house eight times. She says of her workshop, 'This is my constant. Most of the time it feels like coming home. With commission pieces it's a little more like work, but doing my own thing it definitely feels like home.'

Having been a store, the studio has a rugged industrial feel; not the fake, modern industrial feel, but the real 'I've been here a long time' industrial feel. It has rough-sawn roof trusses, steel bracing and bolts, beautiful solid wood floors and timber roof sarking. The high ceiling and sawtooth roof provides a light-filled space and room for a loft that doubles as office space, storage and viewing platform. It was from the staircase that the name of Jane's studio evolved. Being tall herself and having passed the tall gene to her daughter, she was constantly telling her daughter to mind her head as she went up the stairs. After numerous head bangings, Jane erected a 'Mind Your Head' sign on the offending beam and hence the studio was named.

One of Jane's earliest memories is of being taken to an exhibition of Japanese art as a pre-schooler. As a child she was given full rein to indulge her passion for all things artistic, including painting, drawing, jewellery making, pottery and writing. She had a poem published in an anthology of New Zealand poetry entitled *A Cage of Words* at the age of 16, and her continued love of words has seen her extending her writing repertoire to include songwriting. She is the singer in two local bands, Underwire, a heavy rock band, and The Proxies, a Pixies tribute band playing surf punk. 'We're all old teenagers,' says Jane, who recently celebrated the arrival of her first grandchild. However music, while it's an essential part of her, does not pay its way sufficiently to be a full-time career. Jane calls it therapy and says, 'It's great, you can have a good scream.'

In the early days, Jane worked in banks and offices. When her daughter was born she took the leap of faith to go full-time into her art, which was mainly sandblasted glass and sculpting. Her foray into glasswork started when she tried etching using a friend's sandblaster. A summer school course in flat glass techniques and the purchase of a glass etch box saw Jane find her niche in hand-cut mirror mosaics, each one individually designed and made. They are exquisitely fine, but for Jane perfect is not exactly perfect. 'I don't want it to look like it's made by a machine,' she says.

Jane is strongly influenced by the balance and symmetry of Japanese art, especially the work of eighteenth-century artist Katsushika Hokusai.

Each of her pieces are individually named and range from Art Deco works to large circular mirrors incorporating locally collected beach glass. Many of the works on her studio wall are already sold, awaiting delivery, including my favourite, sitting above her desk, entitled *Blue Tidal Flow,* an exquisite blend of mosaic and etching. Despite numerous exhibitions, both solo and group, Jane says, 'It has always been a struggle to get my work accepted as art. Being made an elected artist member of the Academy of Fine Arts in 2004 gave me confidence.' Teaching is something that has also given Jane confidence. Despite her out there 'rock chick' side, she says she thought she'd be too shy to teach, but says she really loves it.

When asked about her favourite pieces, Jane says, 'There's definitely magic about mirrors.' As an example, she recounts the moving story of a mother who commissioned a mirror for her daughter. Having been raped a year before, her daughter was unable to look at herself in the mirror. Jane made her a mirror that was designed to draw the eye from the mosaicked edges into the central mirror. Two weeks after its delivery, the mother rang to tell Jane of an incredible breakthrough: her daughter was looking at herself again thanks to Jane's mirror.

Another story had us discussing synaesthesia, where a person can experience a visual art piece through sounds, touch and taste. At an exhibition Jane had two pieces entitled *Night Music* and *When Ella Sings.* Intended as a pair, *When Ella Sings* was initially sold separately. A few weeks later the buyer returned to Jane to buy the other piece, saying the mirror wasn't singing on its own. This was something Jane could instantly relate to as she has had many synaesthesia experiences over the years, particularly in art galleries.

Jane has an impressive list of commissions to her credit, including mirrors made for Sir Ian McKellen for his New York and London homes, for the British High Commission in Wellington and for the Museum Hotel apartments. She has also sold pieces to numerous private collectors both in New Zealand and overseas. Recently, Jane sold a piece to the James Wallace Art Trust for their permanent collection. The trust was set up to provide support for and to promote contemporary New Zealand artists, and it provides the public access to its culturally and historically significant collection through its gallery in the Pah Homestead in Auckland.

Looking to the future, Jane says she would like to reconnect with sculpture and painting. She has a five-year plan, which includes becoming an artist in residence overseas somewhere, preferably in Spain.

Rebekah Codlin
Picton

A Window to the Soul

I first found Rebekah Codlin's incredibly life-like portraits in a café in Havelock, and was absolutely stunned to find that they were a collection of works by a 22-year-old. The paintings capture the raw emotion and personality of each subject, with subtle colourings and highlights that make the faces come alive. What's more, Rebekah had business cards and brochures to take away, showing a remarkable level of professionalism for someone so young.

Rebekah was raised in Ngakuta Bay in the Marlborough Sounds, a small settlement northwest of Picton. She has never attended school, completing all her studies by correspondence, and I couldn't help wondering if that contributed to Rebekah's incredibly positive and mature outlook on life. Her beginnings with art started, as with many young children, at the kitchen table, with paint and paper. Rebekah first experimented with realism at age 11, painting her brother on a tractor.

At 16, Rebekah started to take her artwork seriously, after she met renowned New Zealand artist Alvin Pankhurst. He encouraged her to pursue her art after seeing a few of her drawings. Spurred on to improve her skills, Rebekah set herself the challenge of completing a drawing every day. She created quick pencil sketches of flowers, boats, scenery, animals and people, training herself

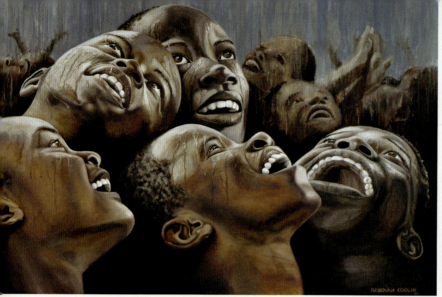

to see the lines and proportions. From pencil sketches Rebekah moved firstly to black-and-white acrylics and then to colour. Speaking of her portraits she says, 'You can't think about your preconceived ideas of what you think the face should look like. You have to observe what is there and nothing else.' Apart from reading a few books, Rebekah is completely self-taught. 'I don't think about technique,' she says. 'Lots of the time I'm on auto pilot.'

Finding the complexity of faces more challenging, Rebekah settled on portraits, and completed her first exhibition at age 17 at Le Café in Picton. Although she kept most of the original oils from this exhibition, it led to a significant number of enquiries for commissions, and later to her next solo exhibition at Terrace Downs Resort in Christchurch. Speaking with the curator prior to opening night, she was astonished to be told, 'We need to price the paintings. We'll put $10,000 on *Storytime*.' At dinner on opening night, the woman sitting next to Rebekah asked her, 'Which painting would you recommend I should buy?' Rebekah replied, '*Storytime*.' 'Oh, that's good,' said her dining companion, 'I've just bought it.' For Rebekah it was just the confidence boost she needed.

Having gained sufficient NCEA credits to go to university, Rebekah had a decision to make — study accounting, or give her art a really good go. Deciding to strike out on her own, she set about finding a number of cafés in the Marlborough area that would display her work. Rebekah approached a local winery, Brancott Estate, and long story short, she now works each Saturday as their artist in

residence. When asked how she felt about painting with an audience, she replies: 'I was surprised how easy it was. It's not really that different from working at home. I enjoy talking to people about what I'm doing. I don't have anything to hide. What you see is what you get. It's also really productive, because all you can do is paint.' This openness and confidence is a refreshing quality in Rebekah. Not many young women recently emerged from their teens have such poise, and I found myself questioning whether the lack of peer pressure and negative feedback from a school environment could have been a contributing factor. 'Correspondence really helped with the creative side and feeling uninhibited,' she said. 'I don't worry about people judging me.'

Although she says her realism has not always gained favour with some people in the art world, Rebekah has quickly gained a reputation for her large-scale portraits, which can measure up to 1.5 metres by 1 metre, and sell for $12,000. Much of her work is by commission, with her paintings selling to collectors in the United Kingdom, the United States, Canada, Australia, Germany, Dubai and New Caledonia. She talks about marketing and working the business side, and credits her mother with pointing her in the right direction. Rebekah sells from her website, and keeps customers updated on Facebook with work-in-progress photos. She has received numerous offers to place her work in galleries, which as yet she has not taken up.

Rebekah's painting studio is comparatively small, a snug 2 by 3 metres, with an amazing view of Picton Harbour. The doors have been removed from the wardrobe to provide easy access to its contents, canvas frames in waiting and poster tubes of her high-quality, limited edition giclee prints. While most of the originals have been sold, Rebekah has kept some, displaying them throughout the house, along with her prints.

On the easel at the time I visited was a large portrait of an African woman. Rebekah starts by pencil sketching the outline, which she then paints in with acrylics. Once she is happy with the composition, she then works in oil, building up the layers until she is happy with the finished painting. Her works can take well over a hundred hours to complete.

On a stand in the corner of her space was a painting of a pair of cheeky African boys, with a glint of mischief in their eyes. Rebekah has completed a number of paintings in her African series, working with a photographer who travels throughout Africa. The images are used as a reference to initiate ideas for Rebekah's compositions. It's the eyes and expressions that capture you. It feels almost as if you are meeting them in person.

Speaking of her room Rebekah says, 'It's my space to focus on what I really like to do. I can close my door and do what I want. It's exciting. There's always something new.' Rebekah also has her eye on the garage. 'I want to convert it into a combined dance and art studio. I'll put mirrors down one wall, with shutters to close them off when I'm painting. I want to paint the outside black or dark brown, and plant mondo grass and sculptural trees, such as lancewoods, to give it a contemporary native look.' You get the impression Rebekah can see the finished studio in her mind's eye.

Rebekah's other love is dancing, hence the combined dance/art studio. 'It's nice to have something physical to do.' She and her sister, Charlotte, have started a not-for-profit dance school called Street Dance Federation, and currently have 85 students. They are also working on a range of brightly coloured dance/street wear, which they were about to launch when I visited.

Christine Boswijk
Mapua

A Room with a View

Imagine for a moment a beautiful tree-lined drive, under-planted with agapanthus, which curves graciously up a grassy hill. There is a glimpse of paddocks and a cluster of buildings, and when you pause, what do you hear? Nothing but the sounds of nature. I'm already entranced with Christine Boswijk's place and I haven't even got up the drive. At the top of the hill is a large courtyard area, to the left a natural timber home set in attractively landscaped gardens and to the right a large workshop area that any bloke would love. But the best is yet to come. Down the wooden side deck you will find Christine Boswijk's studio, which has a view to die for.

    The first thing that captures my attention is the beautiful renaissance-style arched windows and the view beyond them across rolling hills to the Waimea Inlet. It would be easy to spend the whole day just watching the changing view: the sunrise and sunset; the mudflats and reflective water; the daily and seasonal changes. There is a sense of the view being a part of the studio space, almost in a spiritual sense, connecting the creative endeavours inside with the splendour of nature outside. Christine has strong views about nature, which have been a theme of many of her ceramic and sculptural works.

'We are part of nature. We are nature. I'm fascinated by the intelligence of nature,' she says. 'My studio is part Kiwi shed and part Māori meeting house. It is my heart and soul.'

Christine's husband, Patrick Maisey, built the studio and his attached bloke's shed from pine trees milled on the property. In keeping with their love of nature, the outside walls are clad in rough-sawn natural timber weatherboards. The internal walls and ceiling are whitewashed timber sarking, with the polished heart rimu floor adding a warmth and richness of colour to the space. The room is large, 330 square metres, with half the space devoted to displaying Christine's work — large sculptural ceramics and oversized domestic tableware-inspired pieces. The other half of the room is her workspace, with a number of built-in workbenches, a large kiln and an orderly collection of the trappings of her work — large pails of clay and glazes, packing crates, a potter's wheel, and moulds and tools. 'I like men's tools,' she says, picking up a rasp and an archaeology hammer, which are the tools of trade for her current work. 'I like the solidness and the practicality of them.' Christine clearly has a practical as well as a creative brain. There is a set of fishing weights, which will anchor the bases of the new sculptures she is working on.

There is also a church-like feeling to Christine's space, which perhaps resonates with her early upbringing as, in her words, a rebellious and stroppy daughter of a Methodist minister. Christine's childhood was marked by illness, and she spent considerable stretches of time in hospital. 'My way of dealing with it was to be creative, collecting things, and having rock and vegetable gardens. I expressed my intelligence through my hands, rather than academically. As a teenager in Wellington I was attracted to the Bohemian lifestyle. I wanted to be like that, to dress like that and to live like that.'

After a career as a dental nurse, Christine married Dutch-born Eelco Boswijk, who opened one of New Zealand's first coffee houses in Nelson in 1961, which was affectionately called The Chez. Christine became engrossed

in café life — fine dining, musical soirees, live theatre, and the art gallery space behind the café — as well as raising their three children.

When Eelco and Christine went their separate ways, she decided to go to art school in Dunedin. Wanting to study philosophy, but conscious of needing to earn a living, Christine majored in pottery. 'You could sell anything at the time, and it was tangible, something my children could understand.' Christine went on to study in Sydney after winning an Arts Council grant. 'For a time I lost my way. Sydney was trendy and seductive. I felt all these expectations on me, but it felt fake. I looked back to Aotearoa, the mountains and the sea, thought about my age, life and death transitions, and the beauty of imperfection. I breathed this into the clay.' This work was hugely successful and resulted in Christine staying on to teach in Sydney.

Returning to New Zealand, Christine rented a packing shed, creating an apartment and a workshop, with her kiln in a lean-to. 'I was broke,' she said. 'The work I'd made in Australia didn't sell in New Zealand, so I started making tableware.' When creative funding was cut, Anne Rush mobilised the Nelson arts world, creating a professional body of artists who actively marketed themselves. 'It changed the life of creative people. If you were out of the city people could find you.'

Christine has an extensive list of high profile exhibitions, at venues that include Te Papa, Expo 92 in Spain, the Dowse Art Museum and the Suter Art Gallery. Her CV reads like a 'who's who' of the art world, with her work being

commissioned as state gifts, housed in collections all over the world, and winning major awards.

In 2004 Christine was made an Officer of the New Zealand Order of Merit for her services to the arts community, and she hosted Prince Edward at her studio. 'It was an incredibly busy time,' she recalls. 'I had acquired a high profile, but it was still challenging. I couldn't get a job, and I still wasn't making serious money. I had to really work to establish my client base. I just kept doing it over the years, and suddenly forty years have slipped by.'

Over the years, Christine has continually reinvented her creative style. 'After Sydney, I no longer made something and clothed it in glaze. I worked with all the materials in mind. It was like creating a geological structure. It changed my whole way of thinking. Nature has all the answers. I love its raw energy and its imperfections. I gave myself permission to do what I wanted, to make it imperfect.' This theme has carried on into Christine's works today, many of which have a large structural element to them.

'The most rewarding for me, as an artist, is when my work acts as a trigger that goes beyond the physical and nourishes the owner on a day-to-day basis as their life unfolds. I want the viewer to have their own journey. When I have a question, I find the answer through my work. I believe in stewardship. We don't own anything, but we give it our best shot so that we leave it in good condition for the next person.'

Jenny Birdling

No Fixed Abode

Many of us have quietly wondered what it would be like to buy a house bus and travel the country. Jenny and her family have more than thought about it, they've been doing it for the last 30 years. Their home is the quintessential gypsy truck, a 1965 Ford with a plywood body painted in traditional forest green. I caught up with Jenny and her daughter Kaahu in Tasman, where Jenny was temporarily working as a caretaker at the Kina Beach reserve, while awaiting the arrival of her second grandchild in Motueka.

Jenny's first experience of house trucking was at the Nambassa music festival near Waihi in the late 1970s. 'I was absolutely hooked. A few years later my partner and I sold up our possessions, bought a 1953 Bedford school bus from my sister, and set out for Te Puke, hoping to get jobs fruit picking. We had two children, a six-year-old and a one-year-old, and we just packed up and left,' says Jenny. 'It was so exciting.' So began 30 years on the road travelling from one job to another, going in whatever direction suited them. To date Jenny thinks they have spent about 17 years in the North Island and 13 years in the South Island.

During their 30 years travelling they have had four different 'houses'. With a growing family, the school bus was exchanged for a larger Commer bus,

which unfortunately guzzled fuel. It met a rather untimely end in Raglan when it caught fire, bringing out the local fire brigade. 'It was a write-off. A friend gave us an old caravan, nicknamed the Silver Bullet, to use in the interim.' Not daunted by the fire, as many would be, they bought a replacement truck, the 1965 Ford Thames Trader that Jenny still uses today. 'We bought it in Kopu for $1000. It was bright orange, complete with a car salvage hoist, and had "JT's Demolition" written on the side. We took it to Raglan where, with one sheet of ply and a bag of nails each week, we gradually built the body, and fitted out the interior using recycled timbers. That's how the truck got the name Phoenix. It then took another year in Pukekohe to get the motor overhauled and to get all the certification completed.'

Ready to move on they joined the Tinkers and Traders group for two seasons doing the markets and gypsy fairs, where Jenny sold her hand-knitted garments. It was during this time that Jenny found out she was pregnant with her third child. 'I knew it would be a girl and I knew the day she would arrive. I was just a few hours out on the timing.'

Returning to Raglan, they got jobs at the ground-breaking (for its time) Recycle Centre. Jenny delivered her baby daughter, Kaahu, in the bus with the help of a local midwife and with her second daughter, Puna, also in attendance. A couple of years after Kaahu was born, Jenny and her husband separated. Jenny, who retained ownership of the bus, got her HT licence and continued with her dream lifestyle, never considering a different choice.

Kaahu, now in her teens, is still travelling with Jenny and has known no other life. She has taken lessons through correspondence and is sitting NCEA this year. While she enjoys the lifestyle, she is also enjoying staying put for the present, as it has allowed her to attend a sports and recreation course and meet others of her own age.

Jenny's truck has had few modifications since the early days. Stepping onto the fold-up rear deck you are greeted by the family pet, Tam, a blue budgerigar. Just inside the back door, there is a small alcove that leads to the bathroom and over the top of this area is a loft space, which is Kaahu's 'room'. It is a surprisingly large space with a double bed, a sitting area and storage space.

The main living area boasts a six-foot couch, a recycled oak table, numerous bookshelves, a gas cooker and a long kitchen bench. The recycled windows and two-piece barn door provide plenty of ventilation and for winter warmth there is a traditional potbelly fireplace. It's an incredibly cosy space, with a wealth of memorabilia from their travels tucked into the shelves and

pinned to the walls and curtains. Every piece of space is used. When asked if things had to be put away when they travelled, Jenny replies, 'Mostly it stays put. We don't travel fast and the truck is very stable.'

Forward of the living area, over the cab, is Jenny's space, with its cute three-faceted front, multiple windows and ceiling vent. There are pictures on the ceiling, a collection of photos, a basket of her grandchild's toys, and a string of prayer flags. It's an eclectic mix of what's important in Jenny's life.

Jenny clearly has a knack of making anywhere home. Outside the truck are piles of artfully arranged driftwood and petrified wood, which she has collected along the beach, and she is making a path using flat rocks found on the beach.

'Travelling has changed over the years,' says Jenny. 'In the early days if we pulled into a reserve, people used to pull out, not wanting anything to do with the gypsies. Now they come over and start chatting. That's the best thing about travelling. I've made so many wonderful friends. We may not see each other for a few years and then we'll catch up again, and we can pick up the conversation as though it were yesterday. My favourite places would have to be the East Coast and Raglan in the North Island, and the West Coast, Golden Bay and the Catlins in the South Island. We've returned to them over and over again. I love travelling with my home with me,' says Jenny. 'You can just get up and move whenever and wherever you want.'

Bev James
Kaikoura

For Every Occasion

After putting up with the aftershocks from the Christchurch earthquake for two years, Bev James knew it was time to move. Having grown up in Culverden, she was keen to make a new home in a more rural area. When she was offered a nursing position at the Kaikoura hospital, she knew she'd found her new home.

There were very few properties for rent in Kaikoura when she arrived, but Bev feels she lucked out when she was able to rent a house with a large downstairs space to turn into her craft room. 'It was the first time I'd had a dedicated space,' she says. 'I decided to use Mum's old wall unit for storage and picked up the craft table at The Warehouse. With the large ranchslider it's really nice to work down here in the afternoons, which I can do most days, as I usually work the night shift. I've never been a morning person,' she says, 'so it suits me.'

Bev comes from a long line of crafty women. 'My nana was an expert tatter, and my mother tatted and did other crafts as well. My grandmother taught me to make felt and dye wool with onion skins. My great-grandmother made shell dolls and created mirror-image bird drawings and my sister decorates eggs. It's kind of genetic, I think.'

Over the years she has tried her hand at jewellery, quilt making, and creating miniature scenes, but Bev's main love is card making, which is why she was so excited to have a dedicated room. In the centre of the room is a trestle table, which is Bev's main work area. There are multiple chairs around the table as she frequently has friends drop in and craft with her.

Around the walls are numerous storage units that house her incredible collection of raw materials. Bev has every kind of stamp, pen, glue, glitter and card stock imaginable all neatly stored away. In fact, she's probably got more stock than many retail shops. There's a carousel holder for the pens, plastic drawers for card, flowers and ribbons. 'I like to have everything at hand,' she says.

Her favourite storage unit is the set of drawers made by her dad. Bev drew up what she wanted and her father made it for her as a birthday gift. It houses her considerable collection of stamps, die-cut shapes and embellishments. Each drawer is clearly labelled with its contents, which is a giveaway to Bev's organised and tidy working style.

While I was photographing the studio, Bev played around with some card, ribbon and flowers, and within seconds she came up with another idea for a card. As well as working in this eclectic way, Bev says she gets her ideas online, especially from Pinterest or Facebook. She is a member of chat groups, and follows other crafters. She even organises to swap die cuts with other crafters online. She'll cut some of her dies in exchange for die shapes she hasn't got.

Over the years she's made hundreds of cards, nearly all of which have been given away. She particularly enjoys making cards for family and friends where she can personalise the card, and is frequently called upon to create cards for staff at work.

Bev's other love is making miniature worlds, like a Noah's ark scene made in a fob watch. On one side, Noah and his ark are out to sea, and when you turn it over Noah has reached dry land. 'I started making miniature dolls when on holiday once. It rained constantly and I needed something to do. It became a challenge to see how small I could make them.'

The detail of these scenes is incredible. There's a surgical scene, using leftover blue cloth from work, and a Christmas scene. Bev uses clear lipstick tubes to create nursery rhyme scenes, using the smallest sizes of animals and people designed for model railway enthusiasts.

A woman of many talents, Bev also enjoys making costume jewellery. There are silver and enamelled necklaces, and beaded bracelets in a range of bright colours. These days, however, her jewellery making is taking a back seat to her newest love, book folding. Browsing the internet one day she came across book folding and wondered what it was. She bought a couple of patterns online and away she went. The patterns prescribe the exact distance from the top of each page and how long each cut should be. Portions of the page are then folded back eventually revealing a picture. It is an exercise in patience, with many patterns taking hundreds of pages. Bev has just purchased Bookami computer software to create her own designs from photographs. The owl pictured was a gift for her sister and was a fold only, as opposed to a cut and fold, pattern. Nothing is too complicated or intricate for Bev. 'I see something and think I can do that, so I do.'

Jane van Keulen
Hanmer Springs

Stash Palace

Walking through Jane van Keulen's front door is like walking into an Aladdin's cave of embroidery. Everywhere you look there are kits, yarns and finished projects. The wide hallway is lined from floor to ceiling with shelves full of the many embroidery kits Jane sells under her label Stash Palace. It's easy to see where the name came from. Jane has the biggest stash of fabrics, threads and wool I've ever seen. Anyone remotely interested in fibre crafts couldn't help but get their creative juices flowing looking at Jane's stock.

Jane has a larger than life personality. Everything she does, she does with exuberance and enthusiasm. The abundance of stock, the rich colours, the variety and number of finished works, all suggest a lady who is living life to the full.

It's fair to say that Jane's passion and her resulting business has taken over the house. The large dining room table, which now resides in the centre of the lounge, is her teaching and working space. The table is so large that there is room for all the bits — scissors, pens, threads and embellishments, of which there are a large number — to sit in the middle, and still have space for 10 people to work around the sides. Next door in the dining room is another table, which holds books and fabrics, with storage bins underneath. The living room displays the huge range of her work — handmade embroidered animals, art quilts, cushions, dolls and mixed-media pieces.

It all got started when, in a bid to have some quality time with her daughter, Jane's mother suggested they take a course together. They joined a weekly embroidery class and from that first session, Jane has stitched (nearly) every day. She started taking every course she could find, joined the New Zealand Embroiderers' Guild and gained a certificate in embroidery design. Her passion continued to grow, filling the double garage where she started to run her own courses, which then led to the creation of her first embroidery kits.

Four years ago, with a desire to move to a smaller community, Jane and husband Rob moved to Hanmer Springs. Having sold his business, Rob let Jane take the lead, telling her to 'go for it', while he supported her by being the most amazing house husband, cooking meals, including lunches for the ladies attending her full-day courses. Jane required little encouragement and within a short space of time had set up her studio right in the heart of the house.

As you walk around Jane's house, including the two-bedroom guest wing that can be booked for a retreat, you are greeted by her work at every turn — framed embroideries, cushions and throws, and embroidered animals. 'There are over ninety pieces of work on the walls,' she says. 'Rob could tell you what it's like living with an obsessive.'

Beside the wood burner is a rack of threads in every imaginable colour, which Jane has hand-dyed in her laundry tub. 'I buy natural-coloured threads and yarns in bulk,' she says. 'It means I can have any colour I want without holding large stocks, and I can also colour-match different thread types to be used in one piece of work. I really enjoy the dyeing. I used to be a hairdresser so that has helped me understand the dyeing process.' Judging by the splashes of dye in the laundry, which Jane acknowledges will need redecorating if they ever sell, the tub has seen a lot of action.

Jane really does have a lot of stuff. 'I'm a very eclectic person,' she says. 'I'm a maximalist. I like stuff. I'm the messy one.' Jane's jumble of stuff has also filled the garage. Despite her recently emptying 23 plastic bins, the cars are still relegated to the driveway. 'I couldn't work in a space that was totally organised. What I like about my space is it's light, it has great views of the hills, it's in the middle of the house so I feel connected, and in winter the log burner is great, and for quiet days there's also a very large TV.'

The bulk of Jane's sales come from the 30-plus different kits that she supplies to retail shops or sells direct to customers. Many of these start life as doodles with pen and paper. 'I'm never far from a sketch pad. I try to create a

new design each month. I make one of everything I design to make sure I'm happy with it and to take photos of it for the kit. Each kit comes with all the pieces required to complete the project and a full set of instructions.'

Jane's kits include animals, purses, glasses cases, chatelaine sets, brooches, knitting bags, embroidered boxes, tassels, pincushions and wall hangings. There are also special seasonal ones for Easter and Christmas, with a new design created each year. But Jane's real passion is her creative embroideries, examples of which — *Perspective*, *Watching* and *Bats in the Belfry* — sit on her fabric-filled filing cabinet. Jane has received a number of awards at both local and national level. 'I have more ideas than I have hours in the day. In the early days I would wake up in the middle of the night with a new idea, and I would have to get up and do it. Thankfully I've got past that now.'

Building the business hasn't just been about passion though. 'The biggest challenge for me has been becoming more business minded. Prior to moving here I didn't have to make money. Now I have financial goals, stock control and promotion to think about, and I needed a good accountant. I have to have a system for what I'm doing each day, making contact with retailers. When are the next Embroiderers' Guild meetings coming up? What stock am I going to need for them? What new designs do I need to create? But it's my passion. I can work until ten o'clock at night, seven days a week. If I wasn't working I'd just be stitching anyway.'

Jane loves to get visitors, so if you are in Hanmer Springs, don't be shy. Drive up the drive and knock on the door. She'll be really happy to see you.

Kristy Wilson
(Ngāi Tahu)
Hokitika

Carving a Legacy

As a child raised in Hokitika, Kristy Wilson grew up with stories of pounamu — tales of expeditions and favourite pieces, and traditional lore like the story of the taniwha Poutini who turned the Waitaki River into pounamu so that she couldn't be taken back home by her husband, Tamaahua.

Many of these stories were told to Kristy by her uncle, Adam Wilson, and her grandfather, Wereitah Tainui, who was the chief of the Arahura River, so you could say pounamu is in her blood. She recalls, as a child, looking for stones during family whitebaiting and fishing trips up the Arahura River. 'I found my first piece [of pounamu] at age eleven.'

Often referred to as greenstone, nephrite or jade, pounamu is mainly found in the South Westland area of New Zealand. In 1997, the government returned all ownership rights to pounamu to the Ngāi Tahu people making them kaitiaki, or guardians, of the stone. 'I learnt the names and how to recognise the stones when I was young. I was just so drawn to them,' says Kristy. 'I always said I would be an artist when I grew up, and living in Hokitika there was very little else happening in the art world apart from pounamu.'

At 16, Kristy left school, gaining a position with jade factory Jade Carving Ltd just south of Hokitika. The company specialised in creating more 'art

pieces' rather than mass-produced pieces for the tourist market. Working for Stan McCallum, she learnt all aspects of jade carving at a time when there were very few female jade carvers on the West Coast. Stan, who was a well-known fossicker, knew where to go to find the rarer stones, and Kristy has had the opportunity to work on some extremely rare and valuable pieces of pounamu.

Initially, Kristy worked to Stan's designs, koru, hooks and twists, but as her confidence grew she started to create her own pieces. She recalls making a sculpture of a lizard on a rock. 'I drew heaps of designs, but was struggling to draw them onto the rock. They just didn't look right so I went out to my uncle's house. I often go and see him if I need some artistic inspiration. My uncle was a wood carver, and he said to me, "Look into the stone and see what's in it and work with the natural lines." When I returned to work I told myself I wasn't going to think about it or even draw the lizard, I was just going to visualise it. I had to trust myself that it would be okay. And it was. Everything has natural lines and patterns, and I work with those. I don't draw designs any more, I just follow what I see naturally. That's how I work now. I also do a lot of freestyle engraving. It terrifies a lot of carvers, but I love it. I love a challenge.'

Kristy explains the carving process. 'Pounamu is the second-hardest mineral in the world after diamonds. The saws we use for cutting and the grinding wheels we use for shaping are all coated with industrial diamonds,

along with the drill tips we put into the hand piece to carve out the designs. There are many different ways of polishing; all carvers are different and use different techniques. For a high-gloss look you would use a polishing wheel, different grades of sandpaper then buff with tin oxide. A more natural looking polish would be done by hand with water and different grades of sandpaper.'

Kristy's love of pounamu has never waned over the years. 'Yes, it's a job,' she says, 'but it's a passion. Every piece is so different, and there are so many colours. It's really cool to make a piece, and then see someone come into the shop and buy it, and proudly wear it.'

Kristy has worked on many specialist pieces and has particularly enjoyed working on pieces for the New Zealand Army, including replicas of missiles and grenades, and also some large trophy items. Her favourite project, however, was making a 13 cm cross for Pope Francis in 2015.

Kristy was one of the founding members of the New Zealand Jade Artists Society, set up in 2013. At the start, she was the youngest and the only female carver. 'There was a lot of the detail and written work to do. It was so good for me. I met some great people and learnt about setting up societies and writing constitutions.'

Kristy is not just a creative at work; she also likes to paint and make jewellery at home. For the first time, she and her partner, Dion, have moved into a house where she can have her own space. 'I've always had to share his space in the corner of his garage,' she says. 'I used to dream about having my very own lady cave.'

While it is early days for her space, she is already collecting together some special mementos. There is a pounamu axe head with a carved wood handle. The two pieces were gifted to her separately, and Kristy recently put them together to display in her room. In one corner is a space for her jewellery work. 'I like to turn old jewellery into new pieces, making brooches and earrings, mostly for gifts.'

Kristy gains much of her inspiration from her family and the beach, and particularly enjoys creating mosaics with materials she has gathered. In the corner opposite the door is her main worktable, where Kristy enjoys making home furnishings. When I visited, it was temporarily home to a pair of gumboots with a mosaic design made of pounamu and pebbles. The finished pair was entered into the AgFest decorative gumboot competition and was awarded second place.

Kristy also has a large collection of pounamu pieces she has been gifted or collected over the years. 'You wouldn't think these were valuable looking at the outside,' she says. 'Some just look like normal river stones.' There is the milky white inanga pounamu, named after the juvenile whitebait, and flower jade, and the raukaraka pounamu named after the native karaka tree, for its green and yellow shaded leaves. There are many types and colours; all of them are different and all are beautiful.

Jacquie Grant
Hokitika

Hand Cranked

Jacquie Grant's love affair with knitting is just a little different from most. Farming in the Lake Brunner district, Jacquie got interested in spinning wool, but she couldn't knit so she bought a knitting machine. While visiting a friend in Harihari she found a hand-cranked, sock-knitting machine in the barn, which she brought home with her. Being mechanically minded, she cleaned it up but found it was missing a few needles, so she rang a Radio Pacific talkback show and asked if anyone had any needles. As luck would have it, an elderly couple in their nineties answered her appeal and invited her to Timaru to check out what they had in the garage. There were three machines in total, which hadn't seen service since the 1950s when they had been knitting socks for soldiers. As luck would have it, two of the machines turned out to be quite rare, something Jacquie was not aware of at the time. She returned home with all three machines, put them in the shed and forgot about them for a time. Then one day she decided to get them going and started making socks as a hobby. She was soon hooked.

After a while, Jacquie started to actively look for the machines. She placed advertisements in newspapers and when the internet started she was quick to get online. She created a chatroom with 1000 followers in the very early days before most of us had realised the power of the internet.

It was through the internet that Jacquie realised others were interested in these hand-cranked sock machines, particularly in the United States. This led Jacquie to start buying them from the US, refurbishing them, then selling them back into the States again. 'I loved the challenge of restoring them, and I really liked the money.' Jacquie also built up a collection of spare parts and, most importantly, a collection of manuals. For the 200-odd machines she owns, Jacquie has manuals for almost all of them.

Along the way, Jacquie met with a few machines that needed replacement parts that were unavailable. She took the parts to local machine shops, but no one was interested in tooling up to make them. 'They practically laughed me out the door,' she says. 'Then a local guy put me onto a Christchurch firm that had made some tattoo machines for him. I drove up in my pink Mercedes, with my TRANNY number plate. That probably had them thinking before I even got in the door. We discussed making the sock machine parts, and long story short, they created the moulds and started producing the parts. From there it was only a step away to designing and making the whole machine.'

Deciding to test the water online, Jacquie advertised through her chat group, saying she was going to make a limited number of machines. They would cost US$3000 each, and would have to be paid for upfront. She said there would

only be 10 of them made, and they would be delivered within 6–12 months. They sold out within a day. 'With US$30,000 sitting in a PayPal account I didn't have a choice but to get on and make them. Since then I've designed and made another four models, improving them each time. With each new model I make, the first ten are made in bronze as collectors' editions.'

Jacquie soon outgrew her home shed and moved into a place in town. She had also outgrown her ability to keep up with demand for her knitted merino socks. With the hand machines, she could produce a pair in 20 minutes — most people take an hour. Jacquie started looking out for larger knitting machines to keep up with demand. Finding a number of old Lane Walker Rudkin machines, she enlisted the help of some local men to show her how to operate and maintain them. 'I decided if I was really going to get into this, I may as well do the whole process. So in addition to the Bentley Komet knitting machines, I bought an old carding machine, a gilling machine to straighten the wool and a spinning machine to create the yarn. I then hank dye the wool using Dharma acid dyes and it's ready for the knitting machines. I also figured that if I was creating yarn for socks I may as well sell it, so I set up a retail shop alongside the manufacturing space, selling knitting wool and other knitted products such as hats and scarves.'

Jacquie now has eight Bentley Komet knitting machines for sock making.

Also standing against the wall is a large flat-bed knitting machine, which she has yet to get going. 'It's only about thirty years old. It's the first of the electronic models.' That makes it a comparative youngster. Jacquie's oldest hand-cranked sock machine dates back to 1803. But even that is not old in terms of knitting years, with the first known hand-cranked machines dating back to 1540. Jacquie has a number of rare models, many of which would be worth over $10,000 in the American market.

Jacquie's website is well sought out in the United States, with the manuals for many of the machines being available to download for free. She sells her socks through the website and continues to sell her hand-cranked sock knitting machines.

Jacquie is 72. 'At my age you don't have plans for the future. Maybe I'll retire when I'm eighty,' she says.

And if you think Jacquie's life has been busy with her knitting machines, then have a think about this — Jacquie has fostered 76 children, with at least 10 being raised to adulthood. She was awarded the New Zealand Order of Merit for her contribution to foster care. She also spent nine years on the Human Rights Review Tribunal. What an incredible lady, with an incredible space, and an incredible collection. Well worth the visit if you are passing through Hokitika or visit her online at autoknitter.com.

Raewyn Parker
Christchurch

A Story of Dolls

When you knock on Raewyn's front door, not only will you be greeted by Raewyn, you'll also meet the local ladies and their menfolk who sit sedately at home on the antique hallway sideboard. Dressed in their Christmas finery, complete with glasses, feathers, boobs and bows, they make an entertaining display.

Raewyn attended a course in needle sculpting, which was the catalyst for this range of dolls, her old people characters. 'In my head there's a little town with a school teacher, and maybe a garden circle happening, and then of course the ladies need some partners so I added some men.'

This is just a fraction of what Raewyn does. Her Christchurch sunporch studio is home to Red Hen Designs, her online crafting business, which as well as selling finished dolls and fabric bears, includes a large range of quilt- and doll-making patterns, which she sells through her website, and also on Etsy, eBay and Trade Me.

Raewyn, who had initially been a stay-at-home mum when her children were small, had been an English and drama teacher at the local college when she and a friend got together to start the business. When her business partner became ill, Raewyn bought her out and continued on her own. In the early days, she made dolls from other people's designs, but it was not

long before she started creating her own. She would take a basic design and create variations upon a theme, enlarging it or shrinking it. Behind each of the characters is Raewyn's love of story, with her range including dragons, mermaids, angels, cloth bears, rabbits, mice, teenage dolls, rag dolls, and, of course, the oldies.

In addition to these, Raewyn has a range of quilt designs, a beautiful lemon and green one of which hangs on the wall in her workspace, and another in blues and golds creates a comfortable 'come sit in me' chair.

Raewyn's sewing room is not a large space, maybe 2 by 4 metres, considering the volume of work she produces. Her overlocker and sewing machine sit at the far end of the room where she can look out into the cottage garden or to the tree-lined street beyond. It's a lovely spot in the early morning when the sun streams in. Along the northern wall is Raewyn's cutting table, with her computer tucked beside it. It's a small fold-up table but it is also the business table where she does the administration and accounts. From here she looks over a family of animals on the windowsill onto the driveway.

The shelves on the back wall hold a range of fabrics in the crisp, fresh colours of the dolls she calls her 'pretties', which are aimed at the young girl market. There are cards of lace and trimmings, including feathers used to create boas for the teenage glamour dolls. A notice board in the corner is covered in photos, cards and reminders. 'It's a lovely space,' she says. 'I can look at the world and I'm separate from the rest of the house, which is good when people come to visit.'

The patterns, batting and finished dolls are stored in the garage, along with her many boxes of fabric. She's working on her goal of buying only what she needs and selling any excess on Trade Me. 'I like to keep changing things up a bit. I want to have something fresh for people to look at. Sometimes I'll start with a picture, or a curly piece of hair, or even just a yarn, and I'll play around with it, adding bits until the ideas come together. I also belong to an online American doll group. They have quarterly challenges. If you do enough challenges you can then do a free online course. It keeps me motivated and gives me new ideas to work with.'

Raewyn is incredibly organised. 'I have a strict routine,' she says. 'I treat it as a twenty-five to thirty hour a week job. I'm in the sewing room by nine each day, take a break for lunch and then I'm back into it. I diary out what I want to achieve each week, working two to three months in advance. I'll have a ballerina week, a mermaid week, a lavender week and so on. It's always a good plan even if it doesn't eventuate,' she says. 'I also set aside a play week for me to experiment with new ideas and designs. That way I don't have to feel guilty that I'm not producing stock.'

As well as selling online, Raewyn attends the Dunkleys Great New Zealand Craft Shows, travelling with her husband. 'Financially it's a challenge,' she says. 'I have to make it viable to justify keeping it. I have to make money, but I also need to satisfy my creative need. Another challenge working on your own is staying motivated. It's exciting when you come up with good ideas in the middle of the night, but it can get a bit routine when you have an order for fifty bears. But you have to do the work that comes in the door.

'Sometimes I think about a shop with a classroom, but then I'm tied. I have to be there or have staff. I love the time flexibility I have at present. I don't think I could work for anyone again. I wouldn't want to lose my independence.'

Another challenge for Raewyn is promoting herself. 'If I sell a doll overseas, I often find other orders flow in from it. But I have to keep putting myself out there.' For all the challenges Raewyn acknowledges that there are very few times when she hasn't wanted to do it, something that I'm sure many of us would like to be able to say.

Working with a Gallery

Asking a gallery to represent you is a big step. Which galleries should you talk to? Will they like your work? What will they charge? I asked Sally Maguire, experienced artist and owner of Artmosphere gallery in Waipawa, to provide some insight into how to create a great working relationship with a gallery.

Before You Start

Ask yourself what you want a gallery to provide. Galleries are businesses that generate profits from the sale of artworks. They are not there to make you feel good about your work or motivate you to work harder. They will promote your work with the aim of selling it so they can gain a commission, which is generally around 40 per cent of the selling price. The feel-good stuff may be a side benefit but it is not their core business, and should not be part of your decision making.

Choosing a Gallery — Do Your Research

Visit as many galleries as you are able to. You may need to go out of your area as many galleries don't stock local artists.

Ask yourself if your work fits in that gallery. Imagine your potential customer. Are they likely to come into the gallery? Would your work add to the range the gallery sells? (They are unlikely to take work that is the same as something they already stock.) What are their price points? Would their display space suit your work?

Talk to the gallery staff, without indicating you are an artist wanting to place your work. Are they knowledgeable and enthusiastic about the work they stock? Would you feel happy with them talking about your work in the same way?

Making Contact with a Gallery

Be professional. Phone for an appointment with the person who can make the decision. Be flexible about the appointment time and try to fit in around the gallery owner's busy schedule.

Never rock up with a boot load of art in the hope that the gallery owner will have time to view it. Gallery owners are dealing with customers, artists and exhibitions, and are often artists themselves. Their time is precious, and they are unlikely to look favourably on your work if you interrupt their day.

The First Meeting

Be prepared. Select three to five of your very best works to show them. It is often more attractive to the gallery if the works have a common theme. Have back-up photos of other works if needed, but base your presentation on those five works.

Have on hand business cards and a short biography of yourself (one page maximum). Always take an invoice book and your bank account details. You are unlikely to sell anything on the first visit, but if the gallery agrees to stock your work, they will need an invoice with the prices of each work and your bank account details to complete their paperwork. Make it easy for them to take you on.

Pay attention to your appearance. First impressions count.

Be on time. Nothing says 'disorganised creative' more than a lack of punctuality. If you do run late, ring them and let them know you have been held up. Be prepared for them to reschedule.

Be friendly. Yes, you may be nervous, but you know your work best and the gallery will want to know your background. Make it easy for them to strike up a positive conversation.

Building the Relationship over Time

Be reliable. Do what you say you will do. Meet deadlines.

Once your work starts to sell, stay with a similar theme. Suddenly changing to something totally different can stop sales and then you are back to square one. If you do want to change tack, talk to the gallery first.

Listen to what the gallery owner is saying about your work. They are seeing customers interact with your work first-hand. This is valuable feedback.

Be grateful. If the relationship is going well, tell them you appreciate what they do for you. We all enjoy a pat on the back for work well done.

Dealing with Rejection

Do not take it personally. Galleries reject work for a wide variety of reasons: it may not fit with their market; they may not have space; they may have just featured similar work; they may have a long waiting list for exhibitions. It is much better for you to be rejected than for them to take your work and not do it justice.

Keep trying. Just because one gallery says no, doesn't mean others will reject your work. Learn from each appointment. Ask yourself how you could present yourself better next time.

Above all, focus on and enjoy the journey. As an artist you will never arrive at a time when you have finished learning. Today's disappointment may lead to tomorrow's great success. Art is never about ego. It is about creative energy. There will always be new challenges and the excitement of new ideas.

Mary Stevens & Jo Banham

Christchurch

Painting Their Way to a Better Life

By anyone's standards, including her own, Mary Stevens has had a tough life. She was the victim of child abuse, had numerous foster care placements, and was again abused while in CYFS care. She was an unruly teenager, hung out with gang members and has been to jail. When her marriage ended, Mary felt she had hit rock bottom. She had children to care for and was on a benefit. She stopped going out and became a bit of a recluse. She was struggling financially and emotionally, and didn't know who to turn to for help. 'I found it hard to trust people. I had been let down by so many people in my life. I felt judged by others,' she says. As Mary described her childhood, I know without any doubt that Mary is one of the children we hear about that have somehow slipped through the cracks.

Many years later, the memories and the scars are still there but she is breaking the cycle with her own children and grandchildren. She has a positive outlook on life and believes she is well on the road to recovering her self-respect and sense of self-worth. What changed for Mary? She started to upcycle

furniture, taking the discarded pieces that no one wanted, showing them some TLC, sanding and painting them, and giving them a new life in someone's home. You could say it's a metaphor for what she has had to do in her own life.

Mary started out knitting and decorating cakes. 'I liked making things. I got really engrossed. It was a safe place for me. I felt I was doing something for me, something which made me feel better about myself.' When she found a number of discarded mannequins, she painted them in vibrant colours, added upcycled lamp shades and sold them on by word-of-mouth or through Trade Me. When the Christchurch earthquake struck, Mary felt lost. 'I didn't know where my "place" was. I wanted to pick up and run away.' As she looks back, she realises that the earthquake provided an opportunity to focus even more on upcycling as people discarded damaged or unwanted furniture.

When daughter Jo, who works in Youth Justice, was badly assaulted at work for the fifth time, Mary could see her struggling with the stress and the resulting depression. 'I was miserable,' says Jo. After a number of weeks during which Jo was on stress leave, Mary coaxed her into helping her with a table. 'We disagreed on what should be done with the table, but it was a beginning for me,' says Jo. 'Now I love it. I love colour. It makes me feel happy.' Jo's first solo piece was a large cane fruit bowl.

From these small beginnings, Mary and Jo expanded into the shabby chic upcycling business. They buy stock on Trade Me, pick up stuff from the dump or on the side of the road, or are given things. The pair see the potential in everything and have gradually acquired the skills they need to complete their projects. Sometimes they make pieces to order, or they'll make on spec, but always there are their trademark bright colours, an attention to detail and pattern, and a sense of humour. The variety of their work is amazing. Just looking at it makes you happy. There are tables and chairs, including a time-out chair complete with digital clock. There are shelves, lamps, a Buddha, and my favourite — a large rocking horse.

When I met Mary and Jo, their workspace included the porch for outside jobs like cleaning and sanding, and the lounge and dining area for painting and drying. They're a family of five with Jo's three boys so space is at a premium. Jo sleeps in the corner of the lounge surrounded by their work in progress. There were a number of projects at various stages of completion, with a recent arrival, a full-sized mannequin, overseeing the production. She is yet to receive her colours. There is a cabriole-legged table receiving its pattern, and the accompanying multi-coloured chairs awaiting upholstery. On the far wall is one of Mary's original lamps. 'It's not for sale,' she says. 'It's a reminder of how far we have come.'

At the time of our interview, an additional room had been allocated to finished product, which was extensive as Mary and Jo were due to attend their first shabby chic market the following weekend. There's hutch dressers in bright green and blue, a giant Mad Hatter's chair, tables and trays, each of them attractively eye-catching. The market stall will look amazing.

'Doing this has been good for me,' says Mary. 'I've had to go out and buy

materials. I've had to talk to people. The market will be difficult, but I'll feel really good if I can do it.' I can hear the determination in her voice.

Mary and Jo are still on a tight budget. Like most Christchurch renters, the weekly rent takes a large portion of their income. 'Sometimes we have to wait for pay day to buy the next lot of paint, but that's okay,' says Jo.

'Lots of love goes into each piece,' says Mary. 'We've priced it very reasonably. We want people to enjoy buying it, not to feel guilty for spending too much money. I like that our work breaks down social walls. I've met people I would never normally meet, and I can chat to them.'

When asked about how they find working together, Jo responds: 'She'll look at it. I'll say "What is it?" She'll say, "Nothing". I'll reply, "Just say it!" and then we'll discuss it. We've had to learn to work on our communication skills.' From Mary's point of view, she says, 'I feel blessed that my daughter wants to do this with me. There's a lot of love in this house. I'm the happiest I've been in years.'

Hannah Kidd
Methven

Safety Gear Required

If you walk into Hannah Kidd's space, you'd better come prepared. Prepared, that is, with leather apron, gauntlets, welding mask and steel-capped safety boots. There's steel rod, sheet metal, welders and vices. On many levels, it looks like a bloke's shed, but there are no cars, trucks or lawn mowers here, and it's way too tidy. The clue is a larger-than-life metal sculpture of a smartly dressed lady with a poodle — just one of Hannah Kidd's amazing creations.

Graduating from art school in Dunedin with a degree in sculpture, Hannah had tried her hand at a variety of sculpting techniques. On moving to Methven 15 years ago, she held her first exhibition of genetically engineered animals, including glow-in-the-dark rabbits.

Keen to improve her welding skills, she worked for a local engineer. Combining this with fibreglass, Hannah's next show featured glossy fibreglass sheep. She even had a crack at taxidermy, her first piece entitled *Aotearoa Barbie* made from a possum. And yes, she did all the yucky bits, from skinning and gutting it, to dressing it up like Barbie. Eventually, Hannah settled on her current style of large, three-dimensional metal animals and people.

Having had a variety of garages as workspaces, Hannah moved her workshop into the heart of the Methven shopping area. It has a little of the distinctive

odour of an engineering shop, but with the grinding done at home, the space is surprisingly clean.

Hannah starts her creations by drawing a simple silhouette onto her workbench in chalk. She then creates a steel framework, individually cutting, bending and welding all the pieces of rod, laying it up by eye. Even before they have their skin added, these are works of art. The movement contours of the body are extraordinary.

Once the structure is completed, the 'colouring in' begins, usually completed by her assistant Sue, who welds flattened corrugated iron pieces, again individually cut to size, to complete the skin of the animal or person being constructed. The corrugated iron is sourced locally from demolished farm buildings and fences. It is rolled flat, often with the help of Hannah's old truck or her husband's lawn mower, and either spray-painted to the desired colour or left just as it has come off the roof, fence or shed.

It's hard to believe that you could call a metal workshop beautiful but this is a beautiful space. It has high, stained wooden ceilings with exposed beams, and skylights that flood the space with light. There are two entrances, one on either side, with tall, oversized doors, each with a distressed paint finish and attractive wrought-iron work over the windows. This is definitely not your average workshop.

The workshop is divided into two areas: the framework area, where Hannah works, and the 'skinning' area, where Sue works. These are functional areas separated by welding screens and the painting table in the centre of the room. Behind the workshop is a lunch room and above is a mezzanine where Hannah's children hang out after school.

The stair wall provides a great space for a pinboard, which shows the progression of Hannah's

work over the years. She has made horses and people, tigers and birds, and a huge variety of dogs.

'My ideas come from anywhere,' she says. 'Travelling, TV, magazines, advertising billboards. They are slice-of-life images, mainly animals or people.' The subject matter has not changed significantly over the years but the execution has. 'My work has become finer with smaller and smaller pieces,' she says.

At the time of the interview, Hannah was working on an exhibition for the Milford Gallery, entitled *Fantastic Land*. Hannah uses her sculptures to make comment on the way we live, with this collection focusing on the way we live so much of our lives in our heads. It features a shark, some still lifes, and seven Labrador puppies, honey coloured, black and brown. They are cute and playful just like their real-life counterparts.

Hannah was commissioned to create a focal piece for the Re:Start Mall in Christchurch. Entitled *Avonside Drive*, it consisted of four figures, each of them going about their daily business: a man with a lawn mower, a lady feeding cats, a man watering the lawn, and an old lady in a dressing gown peering through her blinds.

Hannah has been in her current premises for three years. 'Having the separation from home is great. I treat it like a job, not because I have to but because I want to. I set goals for the day or the week. Sometimes it's just about coming down and putting the hours in. I listen to audio books and podcasts. It's great, I get to "read" all the books I otherwise wouldn't have: *War and Peace* and *The Luminaries*.' When asked if she had a favourite piece that she has made, Hannah replies, 'My favourite thing is always what I'm working on. I have high expectations of what I am doing.'

There is something very special about her animals. It is like Hannah has breathed a personality into each of them, welding it into their construction, piece by piece, creating a snapshot in time.

These days Hannah works on approximately half-and-half commissions and her own speculative designs. 'Commissions are great when they point you in a direction but then give you free rein,' she says. 'In the future I'd like to maybe do my masters. I'd like to have a clearer vision of what I'm trying to project. But I've got so much stuff I want to make that I can't stop. Yes, there are challenges, finances being one of them. That can be quite a handbrake on me. I have to have a balance between the everyday more saleable items, like the smaller animals, and the more niche stuff that I like to make.'

Sister Annette

Community of the Sacred Name, Ashburton

In God's Name

Five years ago Sister Annette, along with the other residents of the Anglican Community of the Sacred Name in Christchurch's Barbadoes Street, had her life turned upside down. After the first quake, they moved out of the convent building into the neighbouring retreat centre. But with the second earthquake came the red sticker and the Sisters had to move out completely.

For a time the Sisters went their separate ways making whatever arrangements they could. Sister Annette along with three others stayed in Ashburton, with priest friends Heather and Rosalind Stewart, who are sisters of the other kind. When it became clear that the Sisters were not able to return to Christchurch, they set about looking for a special place that would become their new spiritual home. They found it on the outskirts of Ashburton, close to the airport.

On 2 June 2011 — Sister Annette could recall the exact date — she and three other Sisters moved into their new home, with a bedroom each, a large lounge, dining and kitchen, and a double garage, which they converted into their chapel. The home is set in large grounds, beautifully maintained with the help of a gardener, as the resident Sisters are all well into their seventies and eighties, with one even having reached the age of ninety.

The Community of the Sacred Name was founded in Christchurch in 1893, the

same year New Zealand women got the vote. Sister Edith Mellish was brought over from England by Bishop Julius to set up the order, with the focus on meeting the social needs of the time: teaching, home nursing and social work.

Sister Annette found her calling at age 23 and joined the community, training as a teacher and a speech therapist. From her second year as a novice, she worked at St Michael's primary school, teaching five-year-olds, which she describes as rewarding work. In the holidays she would seek out the convent's embroidery room. She recalls her first lesson with Sister Doreen, and the Sister's rather intimidating question, 'Now, dear, do you know how to use a thimble?' 'I'd never used a thimble in my life,' says Sister Annette.

Beginning with the very basics, Sister Annette was introduced to the exacting work of ecclesiastical embroidery. Over the years, she has had many roles within the community: Novice Mistress, Assistant Mother and Mother, but 'I was always happiest with a needle and thread in my hand,' she says.

A good deal was recovered from the convent in Barbadoes Street. The refectory table is now in the dining room, and a small altar graces their chapel. With assistance from the caretaker, Sister Annette was able to rescue the extensive collection of embroidery threads and fabrics from the convent's embroidery room. Many of these would have been irreplaceable, including Filo-floss silk, Jap metallic silver and gold threads still in their original wrappers, and Maltese silk threads in a variety of colours. Many of these are now stored in carefully labelled boxes in Sister Annette's large wardrobe. 'There's plenty of room for them,' she says. 'We don't have much in the way of clothing. Just a few habits,' she says with a twinkle

in her eye. The threads and fabrics, which are clearly very precious, are stored in beautiful old Ballantynes boxes and tins, and would easily fill a double wardrobe. 'It was such a major undertaking to move everything from the convent. We spent days and days packing it all up, and labelling it so that we could find everything once we had a permanent home in which to unpack it.'

Another of Sister Annette's skills is calligraphy, which she learnt from a Second World War airman who had been shot down and badly injured. He was living in Timaru at the time and would teach her and critique her work via correspondence. 'I designed many Christmas and occasion cards for the church. It was lovely to use my skill for the community's benefit,' she says, showing me the wonderful collection of cards printed from her original drawings and calligraphy, completed well before the time of digital printing.

Sister Annette's workspace is at a small table by the window in her room. From here she has a view of the beautiful garden. The desk has her embroidery things neatly placed in front of her. Her papers are pushed to one side. The whole room has a homely feel, with a brightly coloured crocheted blanket on her bed, and floor-to-ceiling bookcases full of books on a myriad of topics. Sister Annette is clearly an avid reader.

When asked about special pieces in the room, she points out a lovely antique table, which is actually a writing desk made by her father. She has the lid propped to a horizontal level so she can use it as a bedside table. She also picks up a small, embroidered needle book. It has been well loved and cared for over her many years of needlework.

Sister Annette has carefully documented her lifetime's embroidery work, taking photos and keeping clippings of the fabrics. A highlight for her was designing and stitching a set of four stoles for the then Archbishop of New Zealand, David Moxon. Some of the traditional designs were based on Celtic designs taken from one of the many books that now reside in Sister Annette's room. A more modern set of stoles was created for a South African priest on the West Coast who asked for the Ethiopian angel icons from her homeland to be included in the design. One of Sister Annette's favourites is a violet stole embroidered with the Scottish thistle, marking the Scottish heritage of its wearer.

Sister Annette particularly enjoys designing embroideries that are personal to the person who will wear them. In the book are also samplers, which Sister Annette and other Sisters have completed over the years as they have learnt new techniques.

There are two women who Sister Annette cites as having influenced her embroidery; the first being Sister Doreen from her early days in the convent, and Jo Dixey (see page 21). 'Jo visited our embroidery room not long after arriving in New Zealand. She helped me find my own craft after Sister Doreen passed away. We still keep in contact today, and another Sister and I have become honorary grandparents to Jo's children. It is very special to me.' Sister Annette also pays tribute to those who have worked with her over the years, especially Barbara Stringleman, Robyn Bascand, and her own sister Beatrice.

At age 83, Sister Annette no longer does the very fine embroidery work involved in making banners, vestments and white work, because of cataracts, but her face lights up when she tells me, 'I'm going to get the second eye operation done later this year. I'm so looking forward to being able to see clearly again.'

At present there are 12 members of The Community of the Sacred Name, many of them from the South Pacific. Much of their work is now in the islands of Fiji and Tonga, and some of the nuns are now back in Christchurch. For the small community at Ashburton, their lives are simple, peaceful, and, above all, prayerful. Theirs are lives well lived.

Madison Drinkall

Woodbury, Geraldine

Watching the Wildlife

When Madison Drinkall reached 18, all she wanted to do was travel. Leaving the mountains and wildlife of British Columbia, she headed for, amongst other places, New Zealand. Having spent her childhood in the backcountry, with a mere 30 people in her village and a two-hour drive to the nearest grocery store, it's not surprising that Madison gravitated to the wilder areas of New Zealand. As many young travellers do, she got a job to fund her travels, working as a cook for a hunting and fishing tour company. That's how she met her Kiwi husband Sam, and she has now become an official resident of New Zealand, living in Woodbury, a not-quite-so-remote area 12 km from Geraldine.

What Madison hasn't done is pick up another 'job'. She's decided to take the step to become a full-time artist, following her passion for graphite pencil sketching. As long as she can remember she has loved drawing, trying a little painting as a teenager, but always coming back to her first love. 'Colour can be distracting,' she says. 'I like the simplicity of black and white. It was also easy to get into. I didn't need expensive paints or equipment.'

Madison's inspiration comes from wildlife in its natural settings. Growing up around grizzly bears, wild sheep and wolves, Madison has a deep connection

with animals, which comes through in her sketches. Her pictures are photographic in their detail, and each animal or bird has a hint of personality to it: a cheeky fantail, a wary rabbit, a soulful spaniel, and a watchful grizzly bear.

'What I love most about being an artist is how it changes your perspective on the beauty of everyday little things. Everything in nature and wildlife has something so precious and stunning about it, you just have to open your eyes and see it. Being an artist teaches you to really see things for how beautiful they are.'

Madison has plenty of New Zealand inspiration. Living on two hectares in the country, Madison has become the adopted mum for a number of foundling animals, with Willow, a red deer fawn, Ziggy, the Arapawa ram, Fern, the lamb, Meg, the chocolate lab complete with eight puppies, and four mallard ducks that took up residence on the pond. She clearly has a soft spot for them all.

The farm had been part of an old forestry block before she and Sam bought it. They have spent many hours clearing rubbish from the property, including the pond. Sam, a builder and helicopter pilot, built their chalet-style home, and while the garden is young it is clear that Madison has an eye for landscaping.

The beautiful rural view from the ranchsliders is easy on the eyes, taking in the paddocks, then across native trees to the hills beyond.

In the corner of the combined kitchen/dining/living area, Madison has her easel. 'I like being amongst it all day in the lounge. It's good to stand a while and look out at the view. Of course, one day I would like a proper studio, but this works well for me now.'

Madison is currently working on a range of New Zealand wildlife. 'I love the deer, the birds, and the plant life, particularly the ferns and the flowers. I still need to get my name out there more in New Zealand,' she says. 'I'd really like to do all the birds in New Zealand.'

Madison often uses photos as a base, starting with a simple outline, gradually building up the shading and detail. 'Every picture I do, I learn something,' she says. 'It's so rewarding to have a light-bulb moment where something finally clicks in my brain and I have learnt a new technique. Another

funny thing I learnt was that if I look at my drawing through a camera on my phone it's like all the bits I've been struggling with or can't see just appear and stick out amazingly, who knew?!'

Madison has been a regular contributor to the Wild Sheep Foundation in America. She has donated prints to their auctions and has found this to be a useful way of getting herself known. After attending a recent show she was surprised and delighted to find her *Home in the Mountains* print had been gifted to the premier of British Columbia, Christy Clark, and was hanging in the state's parliament buildings.

Most of Madison's work is by commission, and she has recently completed a number of pet portraits, including horses and dogs, mostly working from photographs provided by the owners. She also sells her sketches and limited edition prints through Facebook and her website, primarily to the Canadian and American markets at the moment, but she is becoming better known in New Zealand.

As for the future, Madison has plenty of ideas. 'I'd like to create a high-quality home décor range, printing my sketches onto fabric for household decorating items such as curtains and cushions. And I've not long returned from a trip to Africa, so there's an African series to do. And I'd like to take up ceramics, and maybe learn how to paint.'

Gina Tatom
Morven

When the Bell No Longer Rings

Dotted around rural New Zealand are hundreds of small churches, built by the dedicated hands of local parishioners of bygone years. They are built in stone, brick or wood, and like their neighbouring schools were once a focal point of the district. With easier transportation and declining congregations, many of these churches have been sold, finding new lives as homes, bed and breakfasts, gift shops, galleries and workspaces.

It was in one of these small churches, 32 km north of Oamaru, that I found Gina Tatom and her mother, Henrietta. Actually I found them at the Akaroa Market selling their soaps and beauty products, but I met up with them a few days later in their church at Morven.

Henrietta bought St Matthew's church 22 years ago. It was built in 1909, under Bishop Julius's authority, and was the last wooden Anglican church he gave permission to be built in New Zealand. As a place with historical and cultural significance, the church has a Category 2 listing from Heritage New Zealand.

The white church sits in a large, grass section and is graced by a row

of fragrant white roses bordering the path. There are the traditional arched windows and, typical of its time, the church has a high-vaulted ceiling with exposed arched roof trusses, which end with turned wood detailing. The roof and floors are made of natural stained timber providing a rich warmth to the space, which smells invitingly delicious.

Gina's space is well organised, with workbenches and shelves to hold the necessary paraphernalia, but little else has changed as they have deliberately kept the integrity of the original church space. A beautiful lead-light window looks over the altar space and three large chandeliers hang from long wrought iron chains. A church hall that was added around 1928 has also been converted into an open-plan living space.

Gina was born in Christchurch and raised in Queenstown where her parents had antique shops. They lived at Closeburn Station 16 kilometres up a dirt road from town. The family lived an alternative lifestyle well before it became fashionable. They had no television, radio or phone. Being strict vegetarians, they grew their own food, ground wheat for bread and brewed their own elderberry champagne. Gina's mode of transport was a horse, which had been left at their property by a passer-through.

Like many young Kiwis in the early 1980s, Gina waved goodbye to New Zealand and headed to Australia where she bought and sold horses, doing a little hairdressing work on the side. Gina loved to travel. Her quest for excitement led her to the United States, a logical step given her father was American.

While in the States, she became a ski instructor, a pro rider and a horse trainer competing horses all over the United States, and in Spain and Belgium. She also went back to school and gained her cosmetology licence.

Gina returned home in 2015. 'After spending so much time travelling and experiencing different walks of life, I learnt that the grass isn't necessarily greener on the other side after all. I've grown to love and appreciate New Zealand and all it has to offer.'

Initially, Gina thought she would join her mother's soap-making business in the church, but it soon became clear they had different goals and ideas, and to preserve their relationship Gina decided to go her own way with Henrietta's blessing.

Gina starting her artisan business, NZ Soap Star, making high-performance botanically based beauty products from responsibly sourced ingredients. She formed her company in October 2015 with the help of a start-up grant from Work and Income. 'The requirements were really challenging. I had to have a business plan, with finalised plant, equipment, and raw materials quotes, and then I had two interviews.' In the end, Gina was successful in gaining a $10,000 grant, and further assistance for the first 12 months of operation. 'My hard work really paid off. It's given me the opportunity to make a go of the business in a professional way.'

Gina's soaps look and smell good enough to eat. 'I really love soap making,' she says. 'Everything is 100 per cent natural, with as much organic product as possible. I buy from New Zealand, and look for ingredients that are responsibly sourced. I have become really good at researching product and getting a good price. I love thinking, "I wonder what this would be like" then making up something new.'

Gina has a variety of soaps, like the scrubby exfoliating soaps made with pumice, sea salt, sugar or grape seed. The soaps all have a base of shea butter, coconut oil, and olive oil. She then adds mineral spa clays such as activated charcoal, bamboo, French green clay or red clay, to help detox the skin. Finally she adds scent: lavender; ginger and lemongrass; tea tree oil;

or aniseed. Her skincare range includes a natural sunscreen made from oils of manuka, raspberry and rosehip, with aloe vera and witch hazel. She also makes an arnica sports rub and an insect repellent.

Gina sells her products through her website, on Etsy, and travels to markets throughout New Zealand. She is also building up a range of retail outlets. When I met her she was busy getting ready for the Wanaka A&P show the following day, which would mean a 3am start. Speaking of the future she says, 'The sky's the limit really. Eventually I'll get a storefront but for now I'm happy building my brand and creating more products.'

In the meantime, Gina lives in her caravan on site, when she's not travelling in it, and is working hard to build her business in a beautiful, quiet corner of Canterbury. The church bell no longer rings. Apparently, the bells, along with the altar, are removed when a church is sold. But this is not a church that progress forgot. It is alive with activity.

Mary Monckton

Five Forks, Oamaru

Out of the Blue

One of the highlights for me as I've been travelling around New Zealand has been visiting community arts centres. Without exception, they have been great advocates for their local artists. I have three lovely ladies at the Oamaru Arts Centre to thank for putting me in touch with Mary Monckton.

Mary lives in a renovated workers' cottage on a lifestyle block at Five Forks, just 20 minutes northwest of Oamaru. It is a characterful home, which suits Mary's artistic touch. But it was a steep series of wooden steps leading to an attic space that had me really enchanted. Tucked into the roof space, the room wasn't large, but its sloped ceiling and pop-out dormer window created a number of interesting small nooks, each of which serviced one of Mary's creative loves.

To the right, tucked into the corner, is Mary's sewing nook where she has made appliqués and quilts in the past, but these days is more likely to be found finishing the edges of her fabric cyanotype prints. Mary was first introduced to cyanotypes when she attended a mixed-media course at the Wanaka Autumn Arts School. Cyanotypes are one of the oldest photographic processes. Fabric or paper is painted with a mixture of potassium ferricyanide

and ferric ammonium nitrate, and then left to dry in darkness. Once dry, items like flowers or leaves or photo transparencies can be placed on the paper, which is then exposed to sunlight. The paper is then rinsed to halt the chemical process. Not only is the finished print beautiful, but the colour, for me, was absolutely captivating. It is a rich cyan blue, as the name suggests.

Beside the sewing table is Mary's considerable collection of art and craft books. On the other side of the chimney flue is a large hand press, a Trade Me find, which was used for binding old Bibles. For Mary it was a 'can't resist' purchase. One of her other loves is bookbinding. Mary originally did a course with Oamaru traditional bookbinder, Michael O'Brien. The course even included the making of several paring knives used for bookbinding, which along with her other tools are kept in a rather lovely old black box. When she entered a New Zealand Association of Bookbinding Crafts competition to bind a letterpress printed miniature book block, she was delighted to find she had won with her tiny steampunk boxed book.

To the left of the stairs are Mary's paper and printing materials, her paints and brushes, and an assortment of other tools and raw materials that she has gathered over many years. Standing in the corner on top of a lovely set of

antique filing drawers is Mary's latest acquisition, a small print-making press. 'I haven't had a chance to use it much yet, but I'm looking forward to trying something new.'

Mary's main worktable is in the centre of the room where she has full head height. It's also dangerously close to the stairs, so her husband made her a hatch, which she can close down. I must say the idea of being able to shut the world out sounded very appealing to me. When I visited, the table was covered in a number of Mary's paper cyanotypes prints, and her latest project, a mixed-media presentation of her family history. 'I was raised sixty kilometres east of Vancouver, and can trace my family back to Hudson Bay Traders and Swampy Cree, the indigenous people. They were originally fur traders who turned to ranching when the fur trade went into decline.' Mary has a collection of old photos and clippings, which along with pressed leaves and memorabilia are being used to create large mixed-media pages that will be bound in traditional leather. It will be a spectacular family heirloom when completed.

Standing at the table, Mary can look out across the rolling hills through a dormer window, which floods the room with light. The window bay is also home to a comfy chair, which just beckons you to sit down, take the weight of

your feet, and pause a while. Opposite the chair is an art map wall-hanging, which Mary created in paper, called *Metamorphosis*. It is a sobering piece as each of the 100 butterflies represents 10,000 people living with AIDS, and 300 who have died. Mary created this piece after learning that many of the girls she had taught in Zambia had died from the disease. Zambia was also the place she met teacher husband, Brian Monckton. After a short stint in London, he applied for a teaching position in New Zealand. 'That was forty-two years ago,' she says. 'We've lived in Blenheim, Titoki, Patea and Oamaru.'

Alongside *Metamorphosis* is another art map by Mary, called *Walking My Dog*. Mary was introduced to this type of artwork through a fibre arts workshop in Whanganui, and each space created represents a different aspect of family life for her sons. It is clear Mary enjoys creating pieces with personal meaning.

There is something special about Mary's space. Just being there makes you feel wrapped in a creative hug, and her enthusiasm for what she does is infectious. Much of her work is inspired by her love of nature, which had its origins in the wilderness of Canada.

Over the years Mary has tried her hand at quilting, pottery and spinning.

She also bravely went back to high school as an adult student and completed her School Certificate and University Entrance in art. As co-ordinator of the Patea community education programme run by the then Wanganui Polytechnic, Mary says she organised and attended many classes. 'Even if I didn't continue with that pursuit, a little of it rubbed off and went into my next creative endeavour.'

When asked about the future, Mary says: 'I'm very content doing what I'm doing. I can come up here all day. I have a lot of stuff here. I need to use up what I've got and pass some on.'

Sue Wademan
Queenstown

Singing with Life

Through the red door, down the hall and around the corner of the Queenstown Art Centre are a number of artist's studios, one of which belongs to the bubbly and outgoing textile artist Sue Wademan. It's a sunny room with high ceilings, worn wooden floors and a wall of windows and it's a peaceful place for Sue to create her intricate, layered textile pictures.

If you didn't already know that Sue's works were made from textiles, it would be easy to think they were impressionist landscape paintings. On closer inspection, you can see the intricate layering of silks and sheer fabrics, with stitching Sue describes as scribbling.

Sue first started working in textiles when she was introduced to quilt making in the early 1990s. 'I did lots of traditional patchwork workshops, but in between I would experiment with fabrics other than cotton, and create something really different,' says Sue. 'It didn't take long for me to realise that my vision problems would prevent me from excelling at the exacting stitching required for quilting, so I started to develop my own way of doing things.' Sue's vision impairment has been with her all her life and, far from preventing her from doing things, has steered her into the artwork she loves, including

working as a commercial artist and a seven-year stint as a potter. But it was creative textiles and Sue's clever use of colour to express landscapes that saw her building a reputation in Sydney, and tutoring requests that included trips to Japan and Europe.

In 2000, she and Spike decided to move to New Zealand, settling in Queenstown. When asked if it was difficult to give up her burgeoning career in Australia, she replies: 'I gave up the city life for a life in an alpine wonderland, so no, it wasn't difficult, and I've never looked back. Also the Queenstown community is smaller and the world comes to us. The acknowledgement is greater. Instead of being a small fish in a big pond, I am now a big fish in a small pond. I love Queenstown. You don't have to go far to see beauty all around you, constantly changing.' Sue lives on the top of Fernhill in Queenstown, with views over Lake Wakatipu to the Remarkables.

Sue clearly gains inspiration from that view as well as the many places she has travelled to, as much of her work is based around landscapes. 'Initially I became a member of the local patchwork and quilting group, but my work didn't really fit with them, so I joined the Queenstown Art Society, exhibiting with painting artists. It took a while to get my textile art recognised as being a legitimate medium for making art. For proposals to exhibit to competitions such as the New Zealand Art Show in Wellington I would enter my work as mixed media rather than textile art. After winning first prize, gaining the esteemed judge Peter Beadle's support, there was no longer a problem with my "style" of artwork.'

Sue has a long list of art awards and her work is in many private art collections both in New Zealand and overseas, with commissioned work taking up more of her time lately.

Sue enjoys working away from home. 'I've got everything I need here [at the arts centre]. People take you seriously when you have a studio here, and when they do, you take your art practice more seriously.'

Although Sue teaches only once or twice a year now, she still enjoys passing on her skills. 'I spend four or five days a week in my studio. There are so many pieces I want to make, and I have enough fabric for the rest of my life. I've collected so much over the years, and people give me stuff.' On first glance it looks like a jumble of all sorts of fabrics, but on closer inspection you see that Sue's fabrics are meticulously organised with even the smallest scraps being kept.

There is a row of glass cookie jars along the back of her worktable, each holding a different colour of bits, and then there are her many drawers and bins of larger pieces, including the ones marked 'special' that contain the unusual, hard-to-get pieces.

There is a sewing table in the corner for Sue's scribbling with stitch, and a large worktable in the centre of the room. The dark blue walls were bare when I visited, as her work had been moved into the gallery. Everywhere I looked bits and pieces drew my attention: the drawers of beautiful threads, and the rich colours of the fabrics. In the short time that we talked, Sue started to piece together a new work. It was fascinating watching her work, picking up

and discarding or placing the fabrics, working with whatever caught her eye, and seeing her excitement as the piece started taking shape.

Sue, who cites Matisse and Gustav Klimt as inspiration, works in two different ways. 'I can start with a photograph or postcard as a base, to get the outline of, say, mountains or islands, and then the fabric takes over, and I play with the colours and the scene as I see it in my memory. These tend to be the larger pieces. With the smaller pieces, I tend to start with a beautiful piece of fabric, and then another that goes with it. It's like sketching. I build up the landscape piece by piece. This is so relaxing. I can do it through any turmoil. It's almost like turning my brain off.' Sue also works in a more impressionistic style often in reds, calling her pieces *Soul Scapes*.

Speaking of the future, Sue talks about creating some larger pieces just for herself, the way she wants them. 'I've earned my living from my art, and broken out of others' expectations. I've always been ambitious by nature, wanted it more, and worked harder. Now it's my time to do more of what I want.'

New things are also capturing her attention: grandchildren for one and 'I'm learning to sing,' she says enthusiastically. 'Adele and opera. I sang for Christmas in the Park. It felt wonderful being on stage. I think we should have a travelling opera school in Queenstown.' And you get the feeling that if anyone can, Sue will be the one to make it happen.

Karen Rhind

Cromwell

Lavender's Blue

If you are ever passing through Cromwell, take some time out to visit Old Cromwell Town down by the lake. It is a lovely collection of buildings reflecting the early days in Cromwell. In the 1980s, under Rob Muldoon's Think Big projects, the Clyde Dam was built downstream resulting in a significant portion of the historic retail area of Cromwell being flooded by the rising level of Lake Dunstan. It was a controversial project at the time, dividing both the Cromwell and Clyde communities. What retail buildings weren't flooded were, in many cases, demolished because of concerns about safety. However, a few lucky buildings remained on their original sites, some were moved to their current site, and some were rebuilt creating a historic precinct. The area includes stables, a blacksmith, a newspaper and a traditional cottage, to name just a few.

It is a lovely walk down memory lane, with its restored buildings and collections of artefacts. It is also a glimpse into creative Cromwell, as the precinct is home to many local artisans and craftspeople. One such artisan is Karen Rhind, who leases The Tent House, so named as it was the space between two buildings where miners coming into town could pitch their tents. Now it's the sweetest-smelling business in the precinct, selling beautiful lavender products made from Karen's home-grown essential oil.

Karen has grown lavender and made her own lavender products for many years. 'As a child, [like many young girls] I used to pretend to be a witch and make potions,' she says. 'I've always loved gardening. Even as a teenager, I designed a patio area for my mum.'

Karen's first lavender-growing property, Briar Dell, was listed by the National Gardens Trust as a garden of significance. About four years ago, she sold the property and decided to start something a little more manageable. With the beauty of hindsight, she separated her growing and retail areas, with her herb- and plant-growing activities being on her lifestyle block with the family home, and her retail area in the heritage precinct where she manufactures and sells her lavender products.

Karen grows three main types of lavender, all of which she says thrive in the hot stony soil of the Cromwell area. 'I plant *Intermedia Grosso*, a little of *Intermedia Super* and also *Pacific Blue Augustifolia*, though I haven't used the last one for oil. They grow larger here, have more brightly coloured flowers and a cleaner, stronger fragrance, making them ideal for creating good-quality oil.' The plants are attractively laid out in wide-arcing semicircles, and look picturesque even in March after flowering has finished. 'I don't have to do much to them,' says Karen. 'I don't spray the plants, and they're grown in weed mat strips to minimise weeding. I feed them occasionally with blood and bone, and I do have to irrigate them.' Karen also harvests lavender from a friend's property, boosting her own production. 'The flowers start appearing around Christmas, with them

fully in flower in January. Picking usually takes place the first week in February, when the flowers are just past their best. This is when the oil content is the highest. It's a frantic time. You have to wait until the dew has dried, and then pick really quickly, as the oil evaporates with the heat of the day.'

Karen, with the aid of a few friends, harvests the lavender primarily with hand shears, catching the lavender heads in large drop sheets. From there the harvest is taken to local winery Two Paddocks, owned by Sam Neill, where they have a lavender still. The lavender is steam distilled and it takes about half an hour for each vat load to be completed. When the steam condenses and cools, the oil and water mixture separates, with the oil sitting on top. This is then siphoned off and stored in dark glass kegs. Lavender yields are very low, with only 3–4 per cent of their weight produced as oil, so it is an expensive process. Because of the small volumes, Karen says it's not worth setting up to distil her own oil, as the equipment is expensive to purchase.

While there is a market for wholesale lavender oil, Karen prefers to turn her oil into product, which she does at The Tent House. She has the cutest shop, with a small Victorian veranda, complete with flowering plants. Through the back door is a beautiful cottage garden, from which Karen sells her lavender plants and Mediterranean herbs — sage, rosemary and thyme — propagated on her property. Karen also grows a variety of grasses, which she has used extensively in her home garden giving it a distinctly Mediterranean feel with its eye-catching combination of grasses, lavenders and echinacea.

Karen's lavender product range includes soaps, liquid furniture polish, spray cleaner, body oil, facial oil, hand cream, and wheat and lavender bags. All of them smell delicious. 'I really enjoy experimenting with the recipes,' she says. 'I find ideas in books or on the internet and play around with the ingredients, making them as natural as possible.' Karen makes small batches, which are easy to manage in the shop and ensure a continuous fresh supply of product.

In addition to selling plants, Karen's landscaping skills are available for hire. With a certificate in horticulture and years of local knowledge of the difficult Otago soils and growing conditions, Karen is building her reputation as a home garden and lifestyle block landscape designer. It is easy to see why. Her home garden, although still very young, is stunning with mass plantings of carefully chosen plants, which thrive in the difficult climate. 'We have lots of growth in a very short season,' says Karen. 'I really enjoy the creative side of designing a garden.'

Karen is also looking forward to her next harvest of olives from the many varieties she has. The trees were planted when Karen bought the property and are just reaching useful production volumes. There will no doubt be a new range of products available at The Tent House soon. She already has plenty of ideas.

Kylie Matheson
Dunedin

Ever-expanding Journey

The first caravan my husband and I ever owned was a camper type called a Liteweight Expander. We took it everywhere, with a motorbike each on the front and back racks, and two Micron sail boats; one on the car and one on the Expander. We have very fond memories of those holidays, so you can imagination our surprise when we called in to see Kylie and found her 1980 Expander decked out as a creative workroom. It no longer expanded, but it was totally cute and a lovely walk down memory lane for us.

Kylie is no stranger to unusual living arrangements. At age 23, she bought an 11-metre bus and converted it into a motor home. She did the conversion herself, believing her grandfather, to whom she was very close, when he said, 'Nothing is impossible. Whatever you want to do, just do it.' Throwing in her job at Cadbury, Kylie travelled around New Zealand in the bus, along with her cat and dog. She funded her trip selling her work at markets and gypsy fairs: miniature gollies, jewellery made from polymer clay, and painted wood saws.

After seven years, Kylie settled in Napier for a time, still living in the bus,

staying put long enough to feel like Napier was home, at least for the time being. Kylie joined the Taradale Pottery Club. Until then her polymer clay and painting work had been completely self-taught. 'Clay was a natural progression for me,' she says.

As her knowledge of clay sculpture grew, Kylie started exhibiting in local galleries. As her success grew so too did Kylie's dreams of having a dedicated workspace. Deciding the bus was too small to be both home and clay workroom, Kylie bought an Expander caravan from a friend for $500. It had been totally stripped out inside and the folding end panels had been removed with the intention of converting it into a food caravan, but otherwise it seemed in reasonable condition. Again Kylie set about the restoration herself, using as many found and repurposed pieces as possible.

The missing end walls, which had once been aluminium, were remade in ply, the front of which has a striking carved tūī design, created by Kylie. Inside, the pop-out end walls became cupboards — made from scrap from a friend's kitchen-manufacturing business — and bookshelves, home to her book collection and samples of her work. The rear pop-out has a cute leadlight window with a display shelf that houses one of Kylie's original pieces, a ceramic lighthouse.

Along the side wall is a $2 repurposed radiogram, which is now a sink, complete with running water. Under the shelf, a favourite place for her cat to sit, is another op-shop find, an aluminium Air New Zealand food locker now used as shelving, and a pull-out printer's drawer, which houses Kylie's jewellery stamps. The bench provides Kylie's main workspace, complete with pull-out extension and lazy Susan. There are chalkboards providing notes and inspiration, and a display shelf at the front of the caravan, which showcases the ever-expanding progression in Kylie's work. The central worktable folds away when not needed, and in the opposite corner by the door is a repurposed metal locker providing additional storage. Everything is well thought out, with attention to maximising the space and creating a surprisingly inviting and practical workspace.

After spending 10 years away from home, Kylie decided to return to Dunedin. It was to be an eventful trip, with a broken Expander drawbar, the lights going out and needing rewiring, and a wheel falling off. 'By the time I got it home it was a real love-hate relationship,' she says.

The bus and caravan are now parked at her home, which she had bought and rented out before embarking on her gypsy life. 'The bus will probably be sold in the near future. I feel bad that it's not running, but the Expander is here to stay. It's my place of work,' she says. 'I come out here and work a nine-to-four day. That is when I am not going to school.' Kylie is enrolled in a Diploma in Ceramic Arts at Otago Polytechnic. 'It's great,' she says. 'It's giving me guilt-free time to explore. I think my family and friends thought I would grow out of it. But this is my full-time job. I've been self-employed, without any assistance, for eleven years. This is my passion. I come out here in the evenings or the weekends and I can work on new ideas. This is life for me. It's a safe place to explore. With coffee in hand, I put my music on and get into it.'

Kylie recently won the emerging artist category at an Otago Art Society exhibition, and was voted 'People's Choice' in an Otago Potters Group exhibition. Both of these exhibitions have added to her confidence.

When asked about the future she says: 'I love doing what I do. All I want is to be able to pay the bills, work a couple of hours in the garden and take the dog for a walk. Money is not the motivator. Being happy is what's important.'

Jo McCraw
Owaka

Totally stumped

When Jo McCraw decided eight months ago that it was time to move on from her job at Colourplus in Balclutha, she wasn't exactly sure what she wanted to do. 'I needed some time to do something creative and see how it went,' she says, and that's exactly what she did. With partner Rodney's support, Jo quit work and went in search of her creative dream. It didn't take long to find it. In fact, it was right under her nose at her husband's sawmill, between Balclutha and Clinton, where he mills large macrocarpa logs. Seeing all the offcuts got Jo thinking, 'There has to be something I could do with them.'

In a very short time Jo was producing beautiful, chunky stools and tables in all shapes and sizes. 'I wanted to be creative, and it made sense to use what we had on hand.' Looking at the finished product you could easily think that Rodney was making them to Jo's designs, but that couldn't be further from the truth. Once he has cut the timber to length, everything else is down to Jo. The sawmill might seem to be an unusual environment in which to find a woman but, 'Lugging timber around is nothing new,' she says.

Jo says she has always done crafty things. 'I've made things, I've painted, and I got into folk art, but I really love working with the wood. I'm quite happy using machinery and power tools, including the big saws at the mill.'

Jo's initial inspiration came from magazine pictures, but now if she puts a piece of wood aside she knows that at some stage she will come up with an idea for it, like the triangular offcuts from her stools, which she is planning to make into jewellery display stands.

Jo cuts the 'stumps' into shape at the sawmill, where she can be found in action under all the safety gear. Using handmade jigs to ensure accurate cutting, she does all the cutting using a bandsaw. For efficiency, Jo cuts multiple pieces at a time, before resetting the jigs for the next piece. From there it is back to the house where she completes the pieces in their basement garage. 'I like doing the finishing work at home,' she says, and it's easy to understand why. Rodney and Jo live on a hill just out of Owaka, overlooking Catlins Lake with views out to the sea. There are a number of Jo's works in their lounge, where we sit and chat. The waisted tables are Jo's favourite and I can understand why as the narrowed, angular waist reinforces the strong three-dimensional sculptural element. They are a beautiful complement to the décor, which, not surprisingly, features natural timber from Rodney's mill.

Downstairs the garage has been turned into Jo's workshop. She's taken over Rodney's workbench and it is here that Jo grinds the stumps and then sands them until they are really smooth. 'It's time-consuming and tedious work, but it's worth it,' says Jo, 'because the next stage is oiling. I like oiling the best. The wood and the grain come alive. Macrocarpa has such a rich, warm colour, and the variety of grain is endless, making each piece truly unique.'

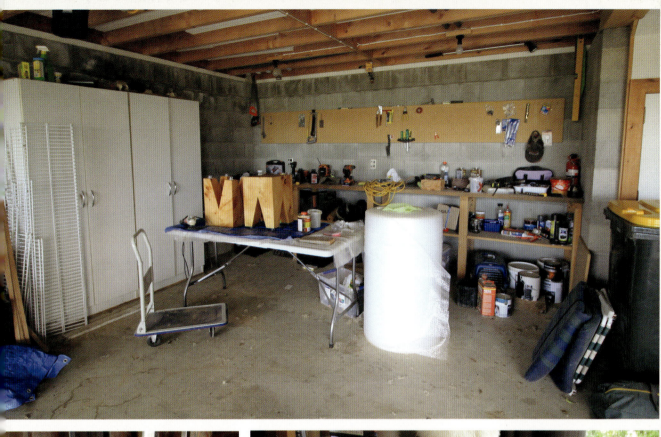

On one side of the garage are the raw cut 'stumps' and on the other side covered in plastic to protect their finish are the completed tables. Jo applies three coats of Danish oil, and the combination of the oil and timber smell is wonderful.

One of the challenges for Jo was coping with the weight of the finished articles. She puts the larger 'stumps' on castors and has now opted for small plastic feet for the smaller pieces. It is important the stools are off the carpet as the timber takes a long time to dry. 'Like most timbers the macrocarpa tends to acquire little splits but that's part of its rustic charm,' says Jo.

Another challenge for Jo has been marketing her finished work. 'I really need a website, but I'm not a technology person. I also found approaching people a bit daunting at first.' But Jo has overcome her natural shyness and now markets in galleries and gift shops in Owaka, Winton, Wanaka and Balclutha. 'It's not really practical to market them too far afield. They're not freight friendly!' she says.

Looking into the future, Jo has ideas of adding metal strapping, creating metal legs or framework for tables, and making butcher's blocks, and no doubt many other works inspired by the stumps at the sawmill.

Laire Purik

Wreys Bush

Halfway around the World

What do kunekune pigs, the beach at Riverton and chickens at a petrol station possibly have in common? The answer is a fair-headed Estonian lady with a wicked sense of humour named Laire.

    A photographer with a difference, Laire is not into the technical details, she's not taking photos of the beautiful South Island landscape, and she's not taking photos of weddings or children. Laire's quirky, humorous photos are a snapshot of the way she sees the world. 'I don't really think about it. I try to do what I'm feeling, capturing a mood or a moment in time,' she says.

    Laire grew up in Estonia, beside the Baltic Sea in northern Europe, at a time when the country was part of the Soviet Union. She remembers the overnight freedom that resulted from the dissolution of the Soviet Union in December 1991. 'It changed my life forever. Suddenly we can travel all around the compass, not just the East as we had been used to. Travel to the West was so exciting.'

Laire packed her backpack and went to see the world: starting with Europe and North Africa before heading south until she ended up in New Zealand. It was on her second visit to New Zealand that she met up with Tomas, from the Czech Republic. They became an item and decided to settle here.

Although Tomas was a trained veterinarian, he was not able to work as a vet in New Zealand without taking further exams, so he was working as a vet's assistant in Riverton when the couple applied for their residency. It would be another four years before Laire and Tomas would finally get their residency approved. 'We certainly found out what is important. It's changed our values in life,' says Laire.

'In communist times, we didn't have much, so we made things.' Laire and Tomas moved into an old farm cottage in Wreys Bush. 'It was June, so wet and cold,' says Laire. 'We put straw bales on the inside of the walls, and added an extra wood-burner. We removed walls to help the warm air move around the house and created a kitchen nook in the living area, making the bench and the kitchen table. We used lots of recycled timbers, leftover tiles, whatever we had, to make the house a home.' Laire is grateful to the local community who helped them get through this difficult time.

Referring to their life Laire says, 'We were living as country bumpkins. It wasn't what we had planned. It was hard not to wonder "why us?" Maybe it's karma. What have we done?' But there is a rustic charm in what they have achieved with so little, particularly in the bedroom where they have installed a potbelly fireplace, exposed the red bricks, and distressed the timber cupboard doors.

It was Laire's fascination with recycled timbers, which she collected wherever she went, that led to her making her first artworks to sell at local markets. Using a decoupage technique, Laire transfers her images to the timber, adding simple but meaningful captions hand stamped onto the timber. They are reminiscent of folk art with a touch of the modern. Each work holds a story, and a hint of humour, like the *Vitamin Sea* boat series. Laire became so renowned for collecting wood, friends would joke, 'Don't let Laire in your house or she'll go away with the fence.'

During the warmer months, Laire's studio is the front bedroom. It is a practical room, with few creature comforts, yet Laire has made it into an inviting workroom. Sitting at her upcycled wooden kitchen table Laire can look out over the veranda and the garden to the rolling countryside beyond and daydream.

Opposite her desk is a large set of windows, which open back onto the lounge, decked with handmade curtains. There is a red and white blouse hanging from a latch. 'I bought it from an op shop. It reminds me of home, only our national costumes are more colourful and have more embroidery.'

There is artwork stacked around the walls and in a wooden drawer, which she uses to transport her pieces to the markets. The space, including Laire's desk, is neat and well organised. Everything is easily to hand. During the winter months though, the room is too cold and Laire moves her work into the lounge area beside the fireplace.

It hasn't been easy for her, but Laire has a positive outlook and her artwork has clearly helped her through a difficult time in her life. 'My first market was at Arrowtown. It was so romantic, and I did really well. I was so happy. I started attending the Queenstown Art and Craft Market regularly, learning from people's feedback. Hearing people's comments helped me a lot.' But it was the words of a local artist that really grew Laire's confidence. 'That stuff shouldn't be in the market,' he said. 'It should be in the galleries.'

'Everyone was so positive, not like at home in Estonia. People were much more critical. It was never good enough. It comes from our history. Life was hard and we had to learn how to survive. It definitely affected the way I see the world. Then I was a dancer, now I'm an artist. Now I have the courage to name myself.'

A recent addition to Laire's range are photographs printed onto natural linen and cotton fabrics. The pictures are rustic, moody and full of emotion. They were added to the range to provide something more easily packed into a suitcase for the many tourists at the markets.

I was lucky to catch Laire at home. She and Tomas were getting ready to move to Stewart Island where Tomas has a job in aquaculture. They will be renting the old whalemaster's house. 'I knew it was the right place when a rainbow appeared over it when we visited in December. It feels a little like home. It has a Scandinavian feel.'

It will be a new start for them both and Laire daydreams about the future. 'I'd like to have a funky boat shed as a studio, or a caravan. Maybe have some accommodation to rent, and I need to set up an online store.' Whatever Laire chooses, I'm sure she will be successful. She is an amazingly resilient and resourceful lady.

Photo credits

All photographs are the work of the author with the exception of those listed below.

Page 15	Bottom left: Liz McAuliffe with large carvings – Lindsay Evans
Page 20	Two photos to the left: Long jacket and fabric-making process – Sandra Thompson
Page 68	Top left: Geppetto, Pinocchio and Jiminy Cricket – Cindy Harvey
Page 99	Middle: *Summer Hugs* and *Winter Kisses* – Jill Matthew
Page 100	*Swish Bubbles* plate – Jill Matthew
Page 114	Diggeress Te Kanawa and Dame Rangimārie Hetet – supplied by Waikato Museum
Page 125	*Kuiwai* – Bernise Williams
Page 126	Anna Korver – Darren Clements (www.darrenclementsphotography.com.au)
Pages 127–8	Studio indoor and outdoor photos – Steve Molloy
Page 129	Left: Sculpting the granite – Jim Howe
	Middle: Finished granite sculpture – Anna Korver
	Right: Sculpting under the canopy – Susie J Lipert
Pages 151–3	Darkroom and artworks – Su Hendeles
Page 156	Left top: Watchtower – Helmut Hirler
	Right: Sally with painting – Helmut Hirler
Page 174	*Rattle Your Dags* by Paula Coulthard and Ursula Dixon – WOW photos © World of Wearable Art Ltd
Page 176	Top left and bottom: Flags – Paula Coulthard
Page 183	*Hermecea* by Jan Kerr – WOW photos © World of Wearable Art Ltd
Page 184	Top left: *Cailleach Na Mara (Sen Witch)* by Jan Kerr – WOW photos © World of Wearable Art Ltd
	Middle: *Quintessentially New Zealand* by Jan Kerr – WOW photos © World of Wearable Art Ltd
Page 195	Pamela Meekings-Stewart – Inspire Photography
Pages 196/7	Middle: Sea view, Right: Altar – Brie Jessen-Vaughan
Page 206	Rebekah Codlin – Brancott Estate staff member
Page 207	Top: *Storytime*, Bottom: *Journey* – Rebekah Codlin
Page 208	Top left: *African Rain* – Rebekah Codlin
Page 215	Top right: Bollard-inspired sculptures – Elspeth Collier
Page 225	Owl book – Bev James
Page 232	Top: Finished pieces, Bottom left: Kristy carving – Tania Wilson
Page 234	Jacquie Grant – Victor Mania
Page 254	Bottom left and right: *Avonside* sculptures – Scape Public Art
Page 262	View – Madison Drinkall
Page 263	Bottom left and right: Bird sketches – Madison Drinkall
Page 276	Bottom: *Soul Scape* – supplied by Sue Wademan
Page 286	Top left: Jo at the sawmill – Rodney McCraw

Acknowledgements

To Bill Honeybone, publisher, and the staff of Bateman Publishing — a big thank you for entrusting me with this project. Your advice and encouragement have meant the world to me.

To Cheryl Smith, book designer, thank you for taking the raw materials, script and photos and crafting them into something that looks so amazing. You are a true creative.

To Nicola McCloy, editor, thank you for making sense of my words and turning them into readable prose.

To Ena Velseboer, friend for life, you gift everyone around you with your compassion, your strength and your zest for living. Thank you for your support and for being you.

Finally to Don Jessen, best friend and husband, I blame you and am grateful to you for getting me into this project. After spending six weeks and 6000 kilometres travelling around New Zealand in a 12-foot vintage caravan, we are still going strong. To say I love you is an understatement of the tallest order.

About the author

Marilyn Jessen has had two outstanding careers. With an honours degree in business management, she carved herself a career in several senior management roles with high-profile companies, before opening her own successful management consultancy. Changing direction, she completed a media arts degree and, following her passion, became a specialist teacher in music, photography and film-making.

Her introduction to books came when successful author and husband Don asked her to take the photographs for his book *Retro and Vintage Boats*, and subsequently for *Vintage and Iconic Aircraft*.